HERBE

Between the Riccall and the Rye

Selected writings on Ryedale
from Herbert Read's poetry
and prose

The Orage Press

*Between the Riccall and the Rye: Anthologized extracts from
The Innocent Eye, The Contrary Experience
and Collected Poems, authored by Herbert Read*

*Published in England in this format by
The Orage Press 16A Heaton Road
Mitcham, Surrey CR4 2BU*

ISBN: 978-0-9565802-1-4

Printed by Lightningsource

Between the Riccall
and the Rye

The Innocent Eye

I

The Vale

When I went to school I learned that the Vale in which we lived had once been a lake, but long ago the sea had eaten through the hills in the east and so released the fresh waters, leaving a fertile plain. But such an idea would have seemed strange to my innocent mind, so remote was this menacing sea. Our farm was towards the western end of the Vale, and because all our land was as flat as once the surface of the lake had been, we could see around us the misty hills, the Moors to the north, the Wolds to the south, meeting dimly in the east where they were more distant. This rim of hills was nearest in the south, at least in effect; for as the sun sank in the west the windows of Stamper's farm in the south caught the blazing rays and cast them back at us, continually drawing our eyes in that direction. But we never travelled so far south as those hills; for the Church and the Market, the only outer places of pilgrimage, lay to the north, five or six miles away. By habit we faced north: the south was 'behind'.

I seemed to live, therefore, in a basin, wide and shallow like the milkpans in the dairy; but the even bed of it was checkered with pastures and cornfields, and the rims were the soft blues and purples of the moorlands. This basin was my world, and I had no inkling of any larger world, for no strangers came to us out of it, and we never went into it. Very rarely my father went to York or Northallerton, to buy a piece of machinery for the farm or to serve on a jury at the Assizes; but only our vague wonder accompanied him, and the toys he brought back with him might have come, like sailors' curios, from Arabia or Cathay. The basin at times was very wide, especially in the clearness of a summer's day; but as dusk fell it would suddenly contract, the misty hills would draw near, and with night they had clasped us close: the centre of the world had become a candle shining from the kitchen window. Inside, in the sitting-room where we spent most of our life, a lamp was lit, with a round glass shade like a full yellow moon. There we were bathed before the fire, said our prayers kneeling on the hearthrug, and then disappeared up the steep stairs lighted by a candle to bed; and once there, the world was finally blotted out. I think it returned with the same suddenness, at least in summer; but the waking world was a new world, a hollow cube with light streaming in from one window across to a large bed holding, as the years went by, first one, then two, and finally three boys, overseen by two Apostles from one wall and adjured from another, above a chest of drawers, by a white pottery plaque within a pink-lustre frame, printed with a vignette of an angel blowing a trumpet and the words:

PRAISE YE THE LORD

Sometimes the child's mind went on living even during the darkness of night, listening to the velvet stillness of the fields. The stillness of a sleeping town, of a village, is nothing to the stillness of a remote farm; for the peace of day in such a place is so kindly that the ear is attuned to the subtlest sounds, and time is slow. If by chance a cow should low in the night it is like the abysmal cry of some hellish beast, bringing woe to the world. And who knows what hellish beasts might roam by night, for in the cave by the Church five miles away they once found the bones of many strange animals, wolves and hyaenas, and even the tusks of mammoths. The night-sound that still echoes in my mind, however, is not of this kind: it is gentler and more musical—the distant sound of horse-hooves on the highroad, at first dim and uncertain, but growing louder until they more suddenly cease. To that distant sound, I realized later, I must have come into the world, for the doctor arrived on horseback at four o'clock one December morning to find me uttering my first shriek.

I think I heard those hooves again the night my father died, but of this I am not certain; perhaps I shall remember when I come to relate that event, for now the memory of those years, which end shortly after my tenth birthday, comes fitfully, when the proper associations are aroused. If only I can recover the sense and uncertainty of those innocent years, years in which we seemed not so much to live as to be lived by forces outside us, by the wind and trees and moving clouds and all the mobile engines of our expanding world—then I am convinced I shall possess a key to much that has happened to me in this other world of conscious living. The echoes of my life which I find in my early childhood are too many to be dismissed as vain coincidences; but it is perhaps my conscious life which is the echo, the only real experiences in life being those lived with a virgin sensibility—so that we only hear a tone once, only see a colour once, see, hear, touch, taste and smell everything but once, the first time. All life is an echo of our first sensations, and we build up our consciousness, our whole mental life, by variations and combinations of these elementary sensations. But it is more complicated than that, for the senses apprehend not only colours and tones and shapes, but also patterns and atmospheres, and our first discovery of these determines the larger patterns and subtler atmospheres of all our subsequent existence.

2

The Farm

I have given the impression that the Farm was remote, but this is not strictly true. Not half a mile on each side of us was another farmhouse, and clustering near the one to the east were three or four cottages. We formed, therefore, a little community, remote as such; in 'Doomsday Book' we had been described as a hamlet. The nearest village was two or three miles away, but to the south, so that it did not count for much until we began to go to school, which was not until towards the end of the period of which I write. Northwards our farm road ran through two fields and then joined the highroad running east and west; but eastward this road soon turned into a road running north and south, down which we turned northwards again, to the Church five miles away, and to Kirby, our real metropolis, six miles away.

The farmhouse was a square stone box with a roof of vivid red tiles; its front was to the south, and warm enough to shelter some apricot trees against the wall. But there was no traffic that way: all our exits and entrances were made on the north side, through the kitchen; and I think even our grandest visitors did not disdain that approach. Why should they? On the left as they entered direct into the kitchen was an old oak dresser; on the right a large open fireplace, with a great iron kettle hanging from the reckan, and an oven to the near side of it. A long deal table, glistening with a honey gold sheen from much scrubbing, filled the far side of the room; long benches ran down each side of it. The floor was flagged with stone, each stone neatly outlined with a border of some softer yellow stone, rubbed on after every washing. Sides of bacon and plum-dusky hams hung from the beams of the wooden ceiling.

By day it was the scene of intense bustle. The kitchenmaid was down by five o'clock to light the fire; the labourers crept down in stockinged feet and drew on their heavy boots; they lit candles in their horn lanthorns and went out to the cattle. Breakfast was at seven, dinner at twelve, tea at five. Each morning of the week had its appropriate activity: Monday was washing day, Tuesday ironing, Wednesday and Saturday baking, Thursday 'turning out' upstairs and churning, Friday 'turning out' downstairs. Every day there was the milk to skim in the dairy—the dairy was to the left of the kitchen, and as big as any other room in the house. The milk was poured into large flat pans and allowed to settle; it was skimmed with horn scoops, like toothless combs.

At dinner, according to the time of the year, there would be from five to seven farm labourers, the two servant girls, and the family, with whom, for most of the time, there was a governess— a total of from ten to fifteen mouths to feed every day. The bustle reached its height about midday; the men would come in and sit on the dresser, swinging their legs impatiently; when the food was served, they sprang to the benches and ate in solid gusto, like animals. They disappeared as soon as the pudding had been served, some to smoke a pipe in the saddle room, others to do work which could not wait. Then all the clatter of washing up rose and subsided. More peaceful occupations filled the afternoon. The crickets began to sing in the hearth. The kettle boiled for tea. At nightfall a candle was lit, the foreman or the shepherd sat smoking in the armchair at the fireside end of the table. The latch clicked as the others came in one by one and went early to bed.

The kitchen was the scene of many events which afterwards flowed into my mind from the pages of books. Whenever in a tale a belated traveller saw a light and came through the darkness to ask for shelter, it was to this kitchen door. I can no longer identify the particular stories, but they do not belong to this period of childhood so much as to my later boyhood and youth, long after I had left the Farm; and even today my first memories easily usurp the function of the imagination, and clothe in familiar dimensions and patterns, exact and objective, the scenes which the romancer has purposely left vague. Perhaps the effect of all romance depends on this faculty we have of giving our own definition to the fancies of others. A mind without memories means a body without sensibility; our memories make our imaginative life, and it is only as we increase our memories, widening the imbricated shutters which divide our mind from the light, that we find with quick recognition those images of truth which the world is pleased to attribute to our creative gift.

3

The Green

The Green, a space of about an acre, lay in front of the kitchen door. It was square; one side, that to the left as we came out of the house, was fully taken up by a range of sheds. A shorter range of buildings continued in line with the house on the right—first the saddle-room, one of my favourite haunts, then the shed where the dog-cart and buggy were kept, and finally the blacksmith's shop. Beyond this were the grind-stones and the ash-heap (in just such a heap, I imagined, Madame Curie discovered radium) and then a high hedge led to the corner of the Green, where three enormous elm-trees, the only landmark near our farm, overhung the duck-pond. On the other two sides the Green was bounded by hedges. The farm-road led past the sheds and then to the left through the stackyard; to the right there was a cart-track leading across the fields to the next farm with its cluster of cottages.

Our dominion was really four-fold: the Green I have just described, and then three other almost equal squares, the one to the left of the Green being the farm outhouses, a rectangular court of low buildings enclosing the Fodgarth, or fold-garth, and two others to the south of the house, the orchard to the east, the garden to the west. Each province was perfectly distinct, divided off by high walls or hedges; and each had its individual powers or mysteries. The Green was the province of water and of fowl, of traffic and trade, the only province familiar to strangers—to the postman and the pedlar, and the scarlet huntsmen. In winter we made the snowman there; in summer avoided its shelterless waste. On Mondays the washed clothes flapped in the wind, but for the rest of the week it was willingly resigned to hens, ducks, geese, guinea fowls, and turkeys—whose discursive habits, incidentally, made it no fit playground for children. The pond was more attractive, but because of its stagnation it could not compete with the becks not far away. I remember it best in a hot summer, when the water dried up and left a surface of shining mud, as smooth as moleskin, from which projected the rusty wrecks of old cans and discarded implements. Perhaps it was a forbidden area; it serves no purpose in my memory.

The pump was built over a deep well, in the corner of the Green near the kitchen; it was too difficult for a boy to work. One day, underneath the stones which took the drip, we discovered bright green lizards. Behind the pump, handy to the water, was the copper-house—the 'copper' being a large cauldron built in over a furnace. Here the clothes were boiled on a Monday; here, too, potatoes for the pigs were boiled in their earthy skins, and the pigs were not the only little animals who enjoyed them, for they are delicious when cooked in this way. Outside the same copper-house the pigs were killed, to be near the cauldron of boiling water with which they were scalded. The animal was drawn from its sty by a rope through the ring in its nose: its squealing filled the whole farm till it reached the copper-house, and there by the side of a trestle its throat was cut with a sharp knife and the hot blood gushed on to the ground. The carcass was then stretched on the trestle, and the whole household joined in the work of scraping the scalded hide: it was done with metal candlesticks, the hollow foot making a sharp and effective instrument for removing the bristles and outer skin. The carcass was then disembowelled and dismembered. The copper was once more requisitioned to render down the superfluous fat, which was first cut into dice. The remnants of this process, crisp shreds known as scraps, formed our favourite food for days afterwards. In fact, pig-killing was followed by a whole orgy of good things to eat— pork-pies, sausages and pigs'-feet filling the bill for a season. But the scenes I have described, and many others of the same nature, such as the searing of horses' tails, the killing of poultry, the birth of cattle, even the lewdness of a half-witted labourer, were witnessed by us children with complete passivity—just as I have seen children of the same age watching a bull-fight in Spain quite unmoved by its horrors. Pity, and even terror, are emotions which develop when we are no longer innocent, and the sentimental

adult who induces such emotions in the child is probably break-
ing through defences which nature has wisely put round the
tender mind. The child even has a natural craving for horrors.
He survives just because he is without sentiment, for only in this
way can his green heart harden sufficiently to withstand the
wounds that wait for it.

On the south side of the Green were two familiar shrines,
each with its sacred fire. The first was the saddle-room, with
its pungent clean smell of saddle-soap. It was a small white-
washed room, hung with bright bits and stirrups and long loops
of leather reins; the saddles were in a loft above, reached by a
ladder and trap-door. In the middle was a small cylindrical stove,
kept burning through the winter, and making a warm friendly
shelter where we could play undisturbed. Our chief joy was to
make lead shot, or bullets as we called them; and for this purpose
there existed a long-handled crucible and a mould. At what now
seems to me an incredibly early age we melted down the strips of
lead we found in the window-sill, and poured the sullen liquid
into the small aperture of the mould, which was in the form of a
pair of pincers—closed whilst the pouring was in progress. When
opened, the gleaming silver bullets, about the size of a pea, fell
out of the matrix and rolled away to cool on the stone floor.
We used the bullets in our catapults, but the joy was in the making
of them, and in the sight of their shining beauty.

The blacksmith's shop was a still more magical shrine. The
blacksmith came for a day periodically, to shoe or re-shoe the
horses, to repair wagons and make simple implements. In his
dusky cave the bellows roared, the fire was blown to a white
intensity, and then suddenly the bellows-shaft was released and
the soft glowing iron drawn from the heart of the fire. Then
clang clang clang on the anvil, the heavenly shower of ruby and
golden sparks, and our precipitate flight to a place of safety.
All around us, in dark cobwebbed corners, were heaps of old
iron, discarded horseshoes, hoops and pipes. Under the window
was a tank of water for slaking and tempering the hot iron,
and this water possessed the miraculous property of curing
warts.

In these two shrines I first experienced the joy of making
things. Everywhere around me the earth was stirring with growth
and the beasts were propagating their kind. But these wonders

passed unobserved by my childish mind, unrecorded in memory. They depended on forces beyond our control, beyond my conception. But fire was real, and so was the skill with which we shaped hard metals to our design and desire.

4

The Orchard

The front garden was formal, like the drawing-room; it was not part of our customary world. If we went there during the day, it was to see if the forbidden apricots were ripening, or to play for a short time round the monkey-puzzle-tree which grew in the middle of a small lawn. But a monkey-puzzle-tree is not a friendly shelter; its boughs are too near the ground, it is hirsute and prickly. The lawn was enclosed by hedges of box, through which narrow arches led to the flower garden in front, to the vegetable garden on the right, and to the orchard on the left. Again, all these provinces were rectangular, without any picturesque charm, but riotous with natural detail, with great variety of shrubs, fruit-bushes and vegetables. The Garden, too, had its shrine. The northern end, in line with the back of the house, was bounded by a high stone wall, sheltering pear-trees. Between this wall and a line of plum-trees, a path, bordered by flowering-currants and honesty, led to the ivy-clad privy. This green retreat, always in memory a place spangled in leaf-flecked sunlight, with ivy-fruit tapping against the small window-pane, has no grosser associations. Its friendliness, its invitation to sociability, was further emphasized by its furniture of two seats, and there we could sit side by side, the needs of our bodies relieved in no furtive secrecy, but in unabashed naturalness.

On the other side, through the wicket that led into the Orchard, there came first the water-trough, an immense stone tank fed from the eaves; this rain water was very precious for washing purposes, so we were forbidden to play with it. It is one of the few memories I have of the sternness of my father, that on one occasion finding me transgressing this law, he immediately picked me up by the seat and immersed me bodily in the water.

Above the trough, high up on the gable of the house, was another forbidden object: the bell which was pealed at midday to announce dinner to the scattered labourers, none of whom was likely to wear a watch.

Behind the saddle-room, in this region of the trough, was the Sand-heap, in a corner formed by a lime house and a low cowshed. The hours we spent in this corner were too habitual to linger much in the memory. It was a generous heap, allowing an extensive system of trenches and castles; near-by was the shade of the apple-trees and the elms; our days there were timeless. Once, playing there, I slipped into the cow-shed to stroke a young calf housed there, closing the door behind me. The calf was lying in fresh clean straw, and did not stir at my approach. Hours later I was missed, and after long searching and much shouting in the farm and the fields, I was discovered sleeping with my head against the calf's warm flank.

The Orchard, like the Green, must have been about an acre in extent. I have no memory of it, except in spring and summer, when the branches, with their succession of blossom, leaf and fruit, met to form an overgrowth supported by aisles of trunks, green with moss or misty grey-blue when the lichen was dry and crusted. One old russet tree sloped up from the ground at a low angle, easy to climb; and in its boughs we shook the blossom till it fell in flakes like snow, or helped ourselves unchecked to the sweet rough-skinned apples. I think the Orchard only held two treasures besides the trees: an old disused roller about which we clambered, and in a far corner, by a bush whose hollow twigs made excellent stems for improvised pipes (in which we smoked a cunning mixture of dried clover and pear leaves), a small trough which usually held rock salt, brown and glassy. In the orchard, and in the paddock beyond, we dug up sweet pig-nuts, and ate them without much regard for the soil engrained in them.

When we emerged from the Paddock, where our pony and the mare for the dog-cart used to graze, there was a sudden sense of space. The ground sloped down gently towards our main stream, the Riccall, which formed the southern boundary of the farm. Beyond the Riccall, which flowed rather deeply in the soft earth and was quite impassable to us, lay a mysterious land we never explored: the south, with the hills rising in the distance, the farm with the fiery windows hidden in their folds.

5

The Foldgarth

The fourth kingdom, the Foldgarth, was the animal kingdom. We usually entered it from the north corner of the Green, and here on the right were the main cow-sheds, the most familiar part of this complex of buildings. Morning and night, and most often by lanthorn light (perhaps it is only the winter scene which is impressed on my memory) the cows were milked in a glow and atmosphere which is for me the glow and atmosphere of the Nativity. The patient beasts stood in their stalls, exuding the soft slightly sickly smell of cow breath; a girl or a man sat on a three-legged stool, cheek against a glossy flank, and the warm needle stream of milk hissed into the gleaming pails. At first it sang against the hollow tin drum of the base, but as the pail filled it murmured with a frothy surr-surr. Here I learnt my first bitter lesson of self-limitation; for try as I would I could not learn how to milk. To manipulate the teats so as to secure a swift and easy flow of milk demands a particular skill; I never acquired it, though my brothers, younger than I, seemed to find no difficulty. This was my first humiliation in the practical affairs of life; another which I might mention here was an inability to make the kuk-kuk noise between the tongue and palate which is the proper sound to urge a horse on gently. These failures in trivial things loom much larger in childhood and affect us much more deeply than any backwardness in learning manners or facts, for they reflect on our physical capacity, and that is much more real to us than any mental power.

Then, along the northern side of the Foldgarth, ran the stable for the carthorses. We were a little scared of these immense noble beasts, for some of them were known to be savage, and ready to bite anyone but the man whose duty it was to look after them.

At the end of the stables a gateway led into the stackyard, and so out on to the road and the fields beyond. At this gateway I once witnessed a terrible scene; an ignorant labourer had taken a pregnant mare out to plough, and by overstraining her, caused a miscarriage. My father and I met him bringing in the horse, with her ghastly trail, and so terrible was my father's passion that he quite forgot my presence as he heaped his curses on the offending man.

My memories of my father are too intermittent to form a coherent image. His sensitive face, his soft brown eyes, and his close curly black hair were not the features of a normal farmer. He loved his farm and was well known for his fervour and enterprise, a tradition he had inherited from my grandfather: he brought some visionary quality to his life and labour. He was a man of austere habits and general uprightness, whose friendship was sought by men of a more recognized intellectual standing. I do not remember that he read much or was in any sense bookish (as I shall relate later, books were scarce in the house). The life of a farmer is hardly consistent with a life of even elementary scholarship, but a sensitive and intelligent mind, in daily contact with all the problems and processes of farming, acquires more than a weather wisdom—an intuitive sense of reality and right values which are not acquired by the mere process of reading.

Along the western side of the Foldgarth ran a line of higher, double-storied buildings. The first was a big hay-barn, open to the rafters, with the pigeon-house built in at the gable end. It was a favourite playing-ground in wet weather: we could make giddy leaps from one level of hay to another; we could burrow into caves and hide completely in its scented warmth. A door at the other side of this barn led to a circular building, with a grinding mill in the middle and a circular track round which a horse could drag the mill-beam.

Then came various sheds for fodder and implements, and over these, approached by stone steps at the end of the building, and outside the Foldgarth, was the granary—a long dry sweet-smelling loft, with bins of golden wheat and stacks of oil-cake, and a store of locust-beans which we ate when we were hungry. A machine for crushing oil-cake stood against one wall, and in this one day I managed to crush my little finger. I fainted with the pain, and the horror of that dim milk-white panic is as ineffaceable as the scar which my flesh still bears.

The other two sides of the Foldgarth were occupied by pig-sties and cow-sheds; the middle by a steadily steaming morass of urine-sodden straw known as the Mig Heap, the infinitely precious store of manure from which the land recovered some of the strength given forth in corn and pasture. The acrid stench of this heap, never unpleasant to any one brought up with it, pervaded the whole of the Foldgarth. The pigeons flocked from roof to roof. An inquisitive calf would lift its head over the low door of its stall. A scurry of hens, an occasional grunt or squeal of pigs, the running of a rope through a ring in the stables: these were the only sounds that disturbed the day's peace, until the men returned from the fields with the weary horses, and the Foldgarth was filled with the clatter of hooves on the stone sets, with the whistling and hissing of the men over their grooming.

On the southern side of the Foldgarth, some of the stables opened outwards, into a lane whose other side was the high wall on the north of the vegetable garden. Here lived the hunters, beautiful pedigree horses which were the pride of the farm— lived in a cleanliness and comfort which put them in a class apart, half-way between humans and animals. I fancy that the fortunes of the farm depended far more on these splendid pampered darlings than on the normal crops and cattle. It was a great day when they were paraded in all their glossy splendour before some horse dealer, and a bargain struck. But sorrow must have been mingled with satisfaction when they left us, and a farm is, indeed, the scene of many sad farewells: pet lambs and ducks stolen away to go to the market with the rest, leaving a broken-hearted child to weep the day away until some consolation is found.

6

The Stackyard

Beyond the Foldgarth lay the Stackyard, looking like an African village, especially after the harvest when it was stored to its limits. The stacks were of two shapes—circular and rectangular—with swelling sides and neatly thatched roofs. The ridges of the rectangular ones were braided with osiers; the round ones were finished off with a fanciful panache of straw. Birds sheltered under the narrow eaves, and would dart out at our strident approach. One summer evening something not bird nor bat fluttered among the stacks; the farm was roused to excitement and the winged creature finally netted. It was a rare Death's Head moth, for which some collector paid the fabulous sum of five shillings. That such riches could lurk in a stackyard was a new portent. We learned that the Death's Head moth was fond of the potato-flower, and the season never afterwards passed without a vain hunt among these despised blooms.

The great festival in the Stackyard was threshing time. Late one afternoon we would hear the chuff and rattle of the engine and threshing machine far away on the high-road, and away we would race to meet it. The owner of the engine, Jabez by name, was a great hero in the eyes of children. He was a small man with a little twinkling face and a fuzzy black beard. He would stop his rattling train and take us up into the engine cabin. I love to this day that particular smell of hot steam and oil which was then wafted to us. With amazement we watched Jabez push over his levers and set the monster in motion. With more chuffing and much complicated shunting the machines were steered into position for work, and then left shrouded for the night.

Very early the next morning we would hear a high-pitched musical hum coming from the Stackyard, and it was with difficulty that we could be made to eat any breakfast. Then we would run across the Green and find round the corner the most exciting scene of the year. The engine stood before us, merry with smoke and steam; the big fly-wheel winked in the sunlight; the bright balls of the revolving 'governor' (Jabez had taught me the technical names) twinkled in a minor radiance. Jabez was in the cabin stoking the glowing furnace. The big leather belt swung rhythmically between the fly-wheel and the threshing-machine. Two men on the top of a stack threw down the sheaves; two others cut them open and guided them into the monster's belly; the monster groaned and gobbled, and out of its yammering mouth came the distracted straw; elsewhere emerged the prickly chaff and below, into sacks that reached the ground, trickled the precious corn. A cloud of dust and chaff swirled round everything. As the stack disappeared, and approached ground-level, we were armed with sticks and the dogs became attentive and expectant. The last layer of sheaves was reached; out raced the rats which had made a home in the bedding of thorns on which the stack rested, and then for a few minutes the Stackyard was an abode of demons: dogs barked, men and children shouted in a lust of killing, and the unfortunate rats squealed in panic and death agonies. Sometimes we found a nest of newly-born rats, and then we were suddenly sad.

I think this festival used to last two or three days; it was our only contact with the Machine God. I suppose we were dimly aware of the railway six miles away, and must have travelled on it, for I know that once or twice we went to Scarborough; but for some reason I have no vivid memory of these excursions, nor of anything associated with them. They were not lived, but pushed without roots into the soil of our daily existence. One curious experience, however, remains with me, and it may well be mentioned here; it is the first of several instances in my life of which I remain incapable of asserting that the experience was of the dream-world. My reason tells me, in this case at least, that it must have been a dream, but the mind does not necessarily assent to its reasoning. I 'appeared' (as we say) to walk down the cart-track that led along the top side of two or three fields towards Peacock's farm; I climbed on to the gate that separated the last field from the high-road, and as I rested there I was terrified by the sudden onrush of a large steam-roller, travelling northwards.

It was distinguished from ordinary steam-rollers (which I had no doubt seen at work on the roads) by the fact that the boiler rested on an enormous bellows, and as the engine roared onwards, these bellows worked up and down and so seemed to throw up through the chimney a fiery column of smoke, steam and sparks. This apparition, which came to me perhaps in my seventh year, remains in my mind today distinct in every detail.

I do not think I was more than usually subject to nightmares (if such this was), but one, which I fancy belongs to a common form, is also remembered by me with peculiar vividness, though it is difficult to describe. I am laid as in bed on a bank of clouds. The sky darkens, grows bluish-black. Then the darkness seems to take visible shape, to separate into long bolsters, or objects which I should now compare with airships. These then point themselves towards me, and approach me, magnifying themselves enormously as they get nearer. I awake with a shriek, quivering with terror. My mother hears me and comes quickly to comfort me, perhaps to take me back with her to sleep away the sudden terror.

7

The Cow Pasture

There was a sandy rankness about the fields stretching towards the river, but these were the main pasture-lands. The Cow Pasture, by far the largest field on the farm, lay on the west of the farm-buildings and its boundary was the western boundary of our land. A path led across the middle of it, and across the neighbouring fields to Riccall House, distinguished from the rest of us by its whitewashed walls and thatched roof. This pasture was rather a godless waste: it was pock-marked with erupted rabbit-warrens, countless mole-hills, and dark fairy-rings in the grass. We implicitly believed in the mysterious origin of these rings, and felt that we might any misty morning find the fairies dancing. Periodically the rabbits had to be decimated, and then fierce dark men with waxed moustaches appeared, bringing ferrets in canvas bags. We would go out in a party, carrying guns and spades, to attack the warrens. The ferrets were loosened from their bags and disappeared down the holes. We listened for sub-terranean squeals, watched for the sudden dart of terrified rabbits, and for the eager inquisitive emergence of the baffled ferrets. The spades, digging easily in the sandy earth, discovered the labyrinths and occasionally a nest of newly-born rabbits.

There was a wide watery ditch on the south side of the Cow Pasture, inhabited by frogs, which spawned among the cress and king-cups. Beyond were narrow fields, running parallel with the river, lush and marshy. The river itself ran between banks, for it was liable to flood over. Eastward it ran for about half a mile, till it disappeared under a bridge which carried the road near Pea-cock's farm—the road of the dream engine. By the bridge was a pool with a projecting pier; this was the sheep-dip, where annu-ally the sheep were given some kind of antiseptic bath.

I remember the oily smell of sheep, sheep-shearing, their ludicrous nakedness when first shorn. Most years there was a pet lamb, a weakling that had to be wrapped in blankets before the kitchen fire, fed from a bottle, and gradually nursed into life. His field would be the Green, and we were his playmates until the inevitable day of parting came. We used to think that the long tails of lambs were bitten off by the shepherd, but actually the animals were gelded by this reputedly safe means. The tails of young colts were cut off with special clippers, and then seared with a red-hot iron. The feet of full grown sheep rot and have to be scraped; maggots burrow into their flesh and pullulate, are gouged out and the sheep anointed. Their wool is infested with nauseous black ticks. Only on the moors, where the sheep are black-faced and agile, with curled horns and quivering nostrils, does this animal acquire any dignity.

The greater part of the Farm was given over to various crops— wheat, oats, barley and rye—and the fields devoted to these spread northwards. Some of them seemed very remote to us. One was sinister, for a large oak-tree grew in the middle of it, and here a man sheltering under it had been struck by lightning and killed. Another field, at the extreme north of our land, had high hedges full of may-blossom; there was a sparse wood on one side; and here, years afterwards when the Farm was only a memory, I staged incidents from the *Morte d'Arthur*.

In the nearer fields we watched the labours of the months. We were aware of the ploughing, the harrowing, the rolling, the sowing, and finally of the harvest. We followed the plough-man, and sometimes ran between the shafts of the plough, pretending to guide it to a truer furrow. At the harvest, as soon as we could walk we became labourers; because then the whole household would turn into the fields, the women to bind the sheaves and pile them into stooks. At lunch-time my mother would drive out with the buggy laden with sandwiches, cheese and bread, and great stone jars of draught beer. We played at hide-and-seek among the stooks, gathered the shorn poppies and cornflowers, watched the field-mice scurry in fright among the stubble and scarlet pimpernel. At the end of the harvest, the last wagon was escorted back in triumph, often late at night in the moonlight, and a great harvest supper was spread in the kitchen, at which my father and mother presided.

In November the hedges were trimmed and layered; the thorns were raked up into great heaps and fired. When we were old enough, my father would have a cart-load of thorns pitched on the Green, and there one night we would dance round the bonfire.

Almost in the middle of the Farm was the fox-covert—a piece of land of perhaps four acres, thickly covered with gorse and scrub, hedged with hazel trees. Twice in a season the Hunt met at our house. They assembled on the Green—the master, the kennel-man and several others in their scarlet coats and peaked caps, the farmers and their ladies in hard billycock hats. The hounds moved in a compact mass, their upcurved tails swaying rhythmically. When the meet was present, they moved off to the fox-covert, and always without much difficulty started a fox. My father rode one of his beautiful hunters; my mother had her pony. At first we children went on foot as far as the Covert and saw them take off, and piped our tally-ho's if we caught sight of the fox. We heard the huntsman's horn as they sped across the fields, waited until we could hear it no more, then went home to wait until the weary hunters returned. But when I was about seven I was given my first pony, and then rode away with the hounds—my first hunt ending in the middle of a hedge which my impetuous pony had taken too rashly.

At the first kill at which I was present I had to be 'blooded'. The severed head of the fox was wiped across my face till it was completely smeared in blood, and I was told what a fine huntsman I should make. I do not remember the blood, nor the joking huntsmen; only the plumed breath of the horses, the jingle of their harness, the beads of dew and the white gossamer on the tangled hedge beside us.

8

The Abbey

Occasionally we made excursions to regions beyond the
Farm. Once a year, perhaps in early autumn, we went
with wagons to some woods eight or nine miles away,
on the edge of the Moors. There we had the right to fell a certain
amount of timber, and to bring it away on our wagons. It was a
long day's expedition, and an immense adventure when we were
allowed to go. We took our food with us and picnicked among
the resinous chips and stripped bark.

This is the only expedition I remember taking from the farm.
My wider explorations were done from other bases. Three or
four times, in times of illness or when, I now suppose, a brother
or sister was expected, I went to stay with relations for a few
weeks. My mother was the youngest daughter in a family of nine,
so we were richly provided with aunts. One of these, a widow,
lived with her two sons and our grandfather in a cottage at
Helmsley, and there I stayed on at least two occasions.

Helmsley was six miles to the west. The road passed through
Harome, a hamlet of white thatched cottages, in one of which
lived a woman, my mother used to tell us impressively, with
twenty-three children. A mile outside Helmsley the road crossed
the railway, and then ran in a straight slope into the town. My
aunt's cottage was on the right as we entered, by the side of a saw-
mill. When a saw was working a high melancholy whine rose
above the houses and filled me with a vague dread. This first
treet, Bondgate, opened into a wide market-place, with a market-
cross and a monument in the middle. On one side the houses were
still half timbered, with overhanging gables; the tower of the
church rose above them, scattering a merry peal from its numer-
ous bells. Once a week, on Saturdays, the market-place was filled

with booths, dense with farmers and their wives. At other times it was a wide deserted space, with perhaps a child or two and a dog at the foot of the cross. Sometimes a cart drawn by bullocks passed slowly across, as if to emphasize an air of almost Eastern sleepiness—such carts being an affectation of the Earl whose park gates were at the end of one of the streets leading out of the market-place.

Beyond the market-place stood the castle with its ivied keep, still massive and imposing in spite of deliberate destruction by the Parliamentarians. Here again was a stage-setting for my later romantic notions, but my authentic memory of this time only associates it with a tennis tournament in which my father took part, and I still see the white figures of the players set against the vivid green of the lawn. Sheep grazed in the empty moats and jackdaws nested in the ragged turrets. The castle might have been more impressive but for still more romantic monuments within my reach. Duncombe Park was an amazing wonderland, which we entered but rarely, and always with an awe communicated by our deferential elders. My eyes searched the wide vistas for some limiting hedge, but in vain. We stopped to stroke a newly-born deer. Vanbrugh's mansion was something beyond my comprehension, of which I only preserve, as fragments from a strange feast, the white ghosts of marble statues incongruous in this greenery, an orange-tree in fruit in the conservatory, and a thatched ice-house. Overhanging a steep valley at the end of the park is a famous terrace, with a lawn as smooth as a carpet and a Grecian temple at each end. Down in this valley is the abbey of Rievaulx.

Rievaulx played an important part in the growth of my imagination, but I cannot tell how much of its beauty and romance was absorbed in these years of childhood, how much built on to these memories in later years. It was the farthest western limit of my wanderings, and so lovely then in its solitude and desolation, that I think my childish mind, in spite of its overweening objectivity, must have surrendered to its subtle atmosphere. One day, years later, I happened to be there when a new church, built under the shadow of the ruins, was consecrated. A choir had come from York Minster, and sang a *Te Deum* between the ruined arches; their sweet voices echoing strangely under the roof of the sky, their white surplices fluttering in the wind. The tomb of Sir Walter l'Espec, the knight who had founded the abbey and had afterwards died as a monk in these cloisters, stood at the end of the chancel. It was not dedicated to any known God, but in a moment of solitude it would serve as an altar to a sense of glory denoted by these ruins and this tomb, and their existence in this solitary place.

Around Rievaulx, and especially through the narrow wooded dales which strike like green rays into the purple darkness of the Moors, I wandered with my cousin, a boy five or six years older than myself. He was a keen collector of birds' eggs, butterflies and flowers, and had great cunning in the pursuit of these objects. From him I learnt how to handle birds' eggs, to empty them through one blow-hole, to pack them in match-boxes. We carried catapults and I was taught the honour of the chase: which birds it was legitimate to shoot, how many eggs one could take from a nest, how to rob a nest without spoiling it or discouraging the mother-bird. One day in mistake I shot a robin, a crime my cousin made more terrible by promising to keep it a secret from the world.

Sometimes we would be out all day, regardless of meals. We gathered wild gooseberries and stewed them in a tin over a fire of twigs. We ate the tender shoots of sweet-briar, sorrel and pig-nuts. I imagine we were severely scolded on our return, but such unpleasantnesses do not endure in the memory. I remember instead the upright figure of my grandfather, white-haired and gentle in his armchair by the kitchen fire, the singing kettle and the cheeping cry of the crickets. We had only candles to light the cottage in the evening. There was a long window full of geraniums, a steep wooden staircase with a latched door that clicked loudly. In this house I have always pictured the story of the Three Bears.

Behind it was a long straggling yard, with outhouses belonging to a builder, and at the end a walled garden where my grandfather grew vegetables and kept bees in straw hives. The privy was here too, and a shed containing, among other junk, some old gas pipes from which I used to try and construct a fountain. I have never met again their pungent metallic smell. Beyond the garden was a lane leading to the cemetery, which with its orderliness and symbolic cypresses was a place very different from the graveyard at Kirkdale. It was usually bright with flowers, and the Sisters of Mercy passed along the gravelled paths with their billowing black robes and white-winged caps. I see now that there was something a little foreign in the whole aspect of this town, with its highly ritualistic church, cloudy with sweet incense, where men and women sat in opposite aisles, its tyrannical vicar, its musical bells, its cart-oxen and its air of seeming to live intently on the four sides of a wide open square.

9

The Church

Every Sunday the dog-cart was yoked up and the whole family climbed into the high seats, my father and mother in front with the youngest of us between them, the rest of us clinging to the precarious back-seat. When it rained an immense gingham umbrella, like the roof of a pagoda, sheltered us all. The big wheels crunched on the gritty roads. The Farm retreated from us as we trotted down the northern road to our parish Church, five miles away. The road had three points of interest: the Little Beck, the Big Beck, and the peacocks. The becks excited us because they had no bridges: they widened out into shallow fords through which the horse splashed as if born to this watery element. In spring the becks were often flooded, and sometimes the water stretched for hundreds of feet in a lake of incalculable depth. Then the excitement was intense, but my father must have known the safe limits of the flood. I remember the water coming up to the horse's belly, and our anxiety for the rug, which had a way of hanging below the footboard.

About a mile before we reached the Church we passed a small village in the middle of which was a country-house known as 'The Hall', and here, on a high wall, we sometimes saw the peacocks which inhabited the garden beyond. For us they were fabulous birds, and the glory of their plumage the most exotic sight of those days. A mile farther on, the road descended steeply into a narrow valley, and there, in complete isolation, stood our Church. First came a row of sheds and stables, where the horse was unyoked and the trap put under shelter. Then the path led a little lower down to the gate of the churchyard, where in summer a few men would be standing, enjoying the air until the last moment. The bell, or rather the clapper, clanged in the squat tower. The Church is of grey stone with a slated roof, and stands out clearly as you approach it against a dark wood of firs. Ancient tombstones lean out of the grassy mounds at all angles. We were taught that it was wicked to walk over a grave, but this grave-yard is so ancient and so thickly populated, that we had to wander as if in a maze. Either before or after the service we made our way to the family graves, at the east end of the Church; but it was not until Mariana died that this duty became a melancholy one, the sight of my mother's tears communicating a wondering sense of woe.

In summer we brought flowers to this grave, and sometimes I was sent to throw away the withered remains of last week's wreath. At the end of the churchyard there was a low wall, and below this a deep ravine in which the river ran, quite over-shadowed by trees. Into this gloomy cavern I threw my handfuls of wisps, glad to hide my uneasiness in this gesture.

Over the porch of the Church is a famous Saxon sundial with an inscription carved on the stone panels at each side which tells us that Orm the son of Gamal bought Saint Gregory's minster when it was all broken down and fallen, and he caused it to be made new from the ground, to Christ and Saint Gregory, in the reign of Edward the King, in the days of Tosti the Earl. Round the dial itself are the words:

THIS IS DÆGES SOL MERCA ÆT
ILCVMTIDE

—this is the day's sun mark at every tide; and below the dial is written: Hawarth made me and Brand the priest.

Inside, the walls are whitewashed, and an aqueous light filters through the foliage-bound windows. The nave was then filled with square box-pews, very high, so that we retired into a little private world, to pray as a family safe from the distractions of less familiar human beings. But the family included our Howkeld relations, of whom I shall soon speak; and my uncle, so patriarchal in his crisp white beard, officiated within our box. He was too stout to kneel on the hassocks which saved our knees from the cold stone floor, but the rest of us, sometimes eight or nine in number, knelt rigidly with hands pressed palm to palm.

The service was of extreme simplicity and dispatch. The sermon never lasted more than ten minutes, sometimes only five.

The music came from a small harmonium, and there was a surpliced choir of perhaps two men and three boys. The congregation numbered in all not more than forty—many less when the weather was wild. In winter the Church was very cold, so we kept our overcoats on, and our breath issued in plumes as we sang the hymns. Once a month there was a Communion Service, and then for a few minutes, when our elders went to receive the Sacrament, we were left in possession of the box, at liberty to fidget and to let our eyes wander to the heraldic monsters displayed on the painted wooden hatchments, to the gallery where the servants sat, and to the trees waving across the leaded trellis of the windows.

After the service (which alternated each week between morning and afternoon, for the vicar served two parishes) the congregation gathered in groups and chatted peacefully as they walked up the path to the gate, and waited for the traps to be yoked up. The inhuman stillness of the situation aided our friendliness; our Church was still where the monks who first built it twelve centuries ago had wanted it to be, in a wild valley, near a running beck, grey like a wild hawk nesting in a shelter of dark trees.

10

The Mill

About half a mile above the Church the beck suddenly slackens; part of its waters (in summer all) disappear down a fissure in the rocky bed. They keep to a subterranean channel for a mile and a half and suddenly reappear, bubbling up from a great depth, at the head of a field which belonged to my uncle, whose small estate was on that account called Howkeld, which means 'springhead'. Here we came often and always with great joy, as to an enchanted kingdom. My uncle was a miller, and the mysterious water, which left its proper course and dived underground as if on very purpose to come up again in this particular spot to offer him its services, ran deep and strong in a willow-fringed bend round the large field separating the mill from the road. At the end of the field it became a walled dam, and to the right overflowed through a sluice into a round lake, which acted as a reservoir for times of drought. The private road to the mill followed the course of the stream and the dam, and then crossed by a bridge under which the water disappeared, combed by an iron grill. It emerged in a swift channel at the other side, and then sluiced in a roaring torrent over the water-wheel. The churned water fell in a dazzling white foaming cascade to a whirling pool below the wheel, and then flowed away with diminishing contortions in a stream which ran round the large gardens and through the fields until it rejoined the mother stream a mile and a half farther south.

There was so much here for childish wonder! The mill itself, with its swinging straps and flickering wheels, the bright chains that hoisted the grain to the top storey, the dusty machines in which we could see, through little windows, the grain trickling, and the general earth-shaking hum and whirr. The foreman's bright eyes twinkled from a face all powdered with flour, his clothes were like white mouse-skin, his beard hoary. His voice was piping high, from having to make himself heard in the din. On Sundays, when the mill was still, flour-dust deadened the sound of our feet on the worn wooden floors; our hands ran sweetly along smooth step-ladders and horny ropes.

Perhaps because there was always a plentiful supply of grain, my aunt kept all kinds of poultry, and in the yard round the mill the most motley assembly of fowls strutted and pecked—not only various breeds of hens, but guinea-fowl, turkeys, ducks and geese. The house was at the end of the yard, T-shaped, its leg in line with the mill. A side door led into the leg, which was a low extension of the original building and here was the Little Room where the family always lived, except on festive occasions. It was a very low room with a varnished wooden beam running across the ceiling. Most of the space was taken up by a sideboard and a large dining-table, and it is hard to think of this room without its comple-ment of food. This was always spread in the most lavish way, with great hams and sirloins of beef, pies, pastries and puddings, and, at tea-time, cakes and tarts of the most alluring kind. My aunt was a famous cook: the mill and the gardens and the farm poured forth their plenty at the doorstep; by barter, in exchange for flour, most of the other essentials and luxuries of life were forthcoming. A deep spring of purest water flowed in the nearest field. War and famine could pass over the land and leave such bounty unaffected.

It was always peaceful here, a peace of guelder-roses and peonies, of laden fruit-trees and patient waters. Perhaps this im-pression means that our visits were mainly confined to the summer; in winter I only remember the frozen lake, on which we learned to skate. People came from far and near on such occasions, and the ice rang with the swift metallic strokes of the skaters' feet. In summer the lake, round which a path led among the reeds and rushes, was given over to the water-hens and wild ducks. Sometimes a flight of wild geese would come sweeping out of the sky on their way north.

I have already described my uncle as patriarchal, and this was true of him in more than appearance. My aunt was the eldest (and my mother the youngest) of the large family I have already mentioned. Some of these had married and migrated to other parts of the world, but such as remained, a goodly number, looked up to my uncle as the head of the clan into which he had married. His stout figure, his crisp white beard and twinkling eyes, his little linen bags of sample grain, his chuckle and his soft rich dialect, were familiar to the whole countryside; and at the time I speak of he was blessed with much happiness and prosperity. But during the next thirty years (he lived to be nearly ninety) he was to suffer many afflictions: the death of his favourite son, the bankruptcy of another, followed by the mortgaging of his own estate and finally a moratorium—and during all these tribulations he remained, a Lear of these Steppes, magnificent in courage and faith.

His children were contemporaries of my father and mother, and this introduced complications into our childish minds, for we called our cousins simply by their Christian names, whilst others who seemed their equals were aunts and uncles. The youngest of these cousins was not too old to despise the part of guide and initiator. One day he organized an expedition to explore the cave at Kirkdale. This famous cave extends for three hundred feet underground, and has more than one branch inside. The expedition, therefore, had to be undertaken with proper precautions. These consisted of candles, a large ball of binderband, and the retriever, Jet. At the entry of the cave we made the end of the band secure, lit our candles, and crept forward unrolling the ball as we went. The sides of the cave glistened in the candlelight; drops of moisture fell from the stalactites above us; the air we breathed was cold and dank. I cannot remember how far we penetrated, but at one point we were terrified by the sudden appearance of two fiery eyes in the darkness confronting us. Could it be one of the ancient hyaenas, not yet a remnant of bones? But it was only Jet, who had run round some loop in the cave and come to meet us.

Once or twice we made expeditions up the dale beyond the cave and the Church. It is one of the wildest and most beautiful places in the whole country; and I still remember my father driving some fine lady from the outer world along the track that went along the ridge of the dale, and how she swore that it was more beautiful than Switzerland, a country of which we had no conception, but which we thought must be wonderful because people travelled far just to look at its hills and dales. This track up the dale ended at a house about two miles from the Church; here the dale became narrower and was filled with thick woods where lilies grew. No road led through these woods, not even a path; but an adventurous spirit could make his way along the bed of the stream, and after a mile or two he would discover that the dale opened out again, to give space to a mill and a few farms and cottages. This is Bransdale, an oasis on the Moors, which in our time only had a poor moorland track to link it with the outer world. The people who lived here were strange and dark and beautiful even to my childish eyes. For sometimes, when staying at Howkeld, I would go out for the day with the wagoners. Our load of grain and flour was drawn by great shaggy-footed cart-horses, their harness bright with brass ornaments, their manes and tails plaited with coloured ribbons—drawn over the wide purple Moors, where God seems to have left the earth clear of feature to reveal the beauty of its naked form, till we dipped down into the green dales and lifted our burden.

The Attic

The successive governesses who helped my mother with our upbringing remain utterly vague to me. They must have occupied a large place in our lives, but except for one insubstantial ghost of dark hair and spectacles, none of them can I recall. I know that they taught us to read, but I doubt if I had acquired that accomplishment before the age of seven. Then books immediately became my element. There was nothing to encourage me in this taste: there were no books in the living-rooms, and my father read little except the *Yorkshire Post* and various agricultural papers. On Sunday he would read to us the lessons of the day (perhaps this was only when it was impossible to go to Kirkdale) and he made us learn the Collect by heart. The only book of his I still possess is *The Poetical Works of Sir Walter Scott*. My mother read to us often, especially *Little Arthur's History of England*, *Evenings at Home*, *Forget-me-not*, and a tendentious story published by the Religious Tract Society called *Little Meg's Children* (by the author of *Jessica's First Prayer*, *the Children of Cloverley*, etc.). I still possess *Little Meg's Children*, and I see now that its grim pathos, too simple to be wholly sentimental, may have worked into the texture of my unfolding imagination, above all to prepare me for the shock of death which waited for me so near; for the first chapter describes the death of Little Meg's mother, and the plight of the orphaned children.

'She turned her face round to the wall with a deep sigh, and closed her eyelids, but her lips kept moving silently from time to time. Meg cried softly to herself in her chair before the fire, but presently she dozed a little for very heaviness of heart, and dreamed that her father's ship was come into dock, and she, and her mother, and the children, were going down the dingy streets to meet him. She awoke with a start; and creeping gently to her mother's side, laid her warm little hand upon hers. It was deadly cold with a chill such as little Meg had never before felt; and when her mother neither moved nor spoke in answer to her repeated cries, she knew that she was dead.

'For the next day, and the night following, the corpse of the mother lay silent and motionless in the room where her three children were living. Meg cried bitterly at first; but there was Robin to be comforted, and the baby to be played with when it laughed and crowed in her face. Robin was nearly six years old, and had gained a vague dim knowledge of death, by having followed, with a troop of other curious children, many a funeral that had gone out from the dense and dirty dwellings to the distant cemetery, where he had crept forward to the edge of the grave, and peeped down into what seemed to him a very dark and dreadful depth. When little Meg told him Mother was dead, and lifted him up to kneel on the bedside, and kiss her icy lips for the last time, his childish heart was filled with an awe which almost made him shrink from the sight of that familiar face, scarcely whiter or more sunken now than it had been for many a day past. . . .'

We must have wept often over the tribulations of Little Meg, and may have been duly impressed by her Christian constancy. Were we held by anything but the pathos of the story? This strange country of dingy streets and attics (an attic perhaps I could visualize), of lack of bread and clothes, of evil and misery—it was as fairy-like as any story that I had heard—as hard to realize, but just as easy to believe. The emotions were involved, and the imagination, but nothing like reflection or reasoning. We were moved in exactly the same way, and perhaps even to a greater degree, by the adventures of Little Red Riding-hood. Both she and Meg were 'Little', and both survived the perils they encountered. When even the perils we ourselves encounter as children leave so little impression on our sensibility (just because we have no reasoning power to trace their consequences) why should the fictitious pathos of a story have more effect? The perturbations of the intellect are a danger to the instinctive basis of life; no wonder, then, that nature is wise enough to wrap us in a cocoon of insensibility, until such time as we have the power to counter intelligence with deeper intuitions.

THE ATTIC

Little Meg's attic could be visualized because we had our own attic at the top of the house. It was approached by a steep staircase just outside the nursery door. On the left, when you reached the top, were two bedrooms, partitioned off and occupied by the maids. But the rest of the space under the roof was free. One side was used for storing apples, and their musty sweetness pervaded the whole room. There were several chests and wardrobes, full of old wedding-dresses, and many other things which I do not distinctly remember. But here also was the only considerable store of books in the house, a miscellaneous collection of foxed volumes of sermons and devotional works which can have had little appeal to me, but which I pored over with an instinctive love. But two larger tomes were an inexhaustible mine of delight. They were bound volumes of the *Illustrated London News* for the year of the Great Exhibition (presumably 1850), full of the steel engravings of the period.

My lust for books was not satisfied in the attic; I soon craved for novelty. But I must have realized thus early that such a longing was a personal affair, to be fulfilled only by a personal effort. Looking round for a means to this end, I seized on the postman as the only link with the printed world. He came daily on his long pedestrian round, for if there were no letters to bring, there was always the *Yorkshire Post*. I made friends with him, and confided to him my secret desires. He was sympathetic, but his acquaintance with literature was limited. It was limited, in fact, to a lurid pink periodical called, I think, *The Police Gazette*, and this he passed on to me; but though I remember the act of reading it, it left no particular impression on me. Evidently its contents had nothing of the reality of a fairy world.

I return again and again, in retrospection, to this early untutored interest in books, for how could it have developed, in such isolation and such neglect, but for the presence of some inborn disposition. And faith in such a disposition becomes, with the growth of the personality, a controlling factor. We are only happy so long as our life expands in ever widening circles from the upward gush of our early impulses; and even love, of which the child is ignorant, is only real in so far as it is a transformation, in adolescence, of our first instinctive attachments.

12

The Musical Box

One day my father brought a delightful toy back from Northallerton: it was a small musical box which played 'For there's nae luck about the house'. But my mother, perhaps then, or perhaps shortly afterwards, when there was sufficient cause, thought the tune was ominous. My only sister was a baby then, between two and three years old. Our farm was called the Grange, and though it had no moat, this daughter was christened Mariana. Perhaps that too was ominous, for a sad song goes by her name. Mariana was fair as sunlight, and smiled to the tinkle of the musical box. And that is all I remember of her, for that spring I was suddenly sent away. A few days later my aunt told me that Mariana had become an angel, and the next time we went to Kirkdale I was taken to see the unmeaning mound that covered her body.

Apart from this fatal musical box, the only other music I ever heard in my childhood was Fiddler Dick's. Every year the young horses bred on the Farm had to be 'broken in', and this was work for a specialist, who, like the blacksmith, paid us periodical visits. Fiddler Dick was a natty little man, with a hot swarthy complexion and waxed moustaches—probably he was of gipsy blood. He would stay a few days at the Farm, sleeping in the loft above the saddle-room. He always brought his fiddle with him, and after dinner, or in the evening, used to play to a wondering audience. I was fascinated by this man—fascinated when he stood in the Cow Pasture, his neat leggings winking in the sunshine, a wild young colt galloping, trotting, walking in a circle at the end of a long rope, controlled by Fiddler Dick's flicking whip—still more fascinated when the brown fiddle came out of its box and a sound, never imagined before, was conjured out of the air. Now,

THE MUSICAL BOX

I had seen, in a chest in the attic, just such a brown fiddle, and one day when Fiddler Dick was at the Farm, I brought it down and asked him to teach me to make such music. But some of the strings were broken, and the bow had no horse-hair. Some untwisted binder-band served to repair the bow, and we got some cat-gut from the nearest cobbler for the strings. Fiddler Dick rejoiced in the word cat-gut, and cats took on a new significance for me. I cannot now believe that the sounds which issued from this improvised instrument bore any resemblance to the plaintive voice of a violin, but I retained my longing to play. Later, when I went away to school, I persuaded my mother to let me take music as an extra subject, and she consented. But I was put to the piano, which had no charm for me, no urgency of aspiration. I could not rival Fiddler Dick on such an instrument! Besides, instead of Fiddler Dick, I had for a teacher a fierce Dutchman, bristling with long hair and a silk bow-tie, flashing with rings. At the end of the year my enthusiasm had so waned that I could not urge my mother to pay the extra fees for music. But I still clung to the old violin, with the vague hope that I might one day learn to play it. It was still in my possession at the beginning of the war, but my mother died at this time, and in the subsequent confusion the violin disappeared. I had expected to find it among the few possessions I had stored in a cellar against my return, but it was not there. I should perhaps never have given it another thought but for an experience of several years later. I came late one evening, after a walk along a forest road in Bavaria, the moon staring at me through the cage bars of the trees, to a large castle where many guests were being entertained. Supper was finished and there was not a soul to be seen, except a porter who took my bag, and told me that everyone was in the music-room—even the servants— and that I had better make my way there and wait for the end. I was directed to a small balcony, which I could enter without disturbing the audience. The room was in darkness, except for an electric lamp at the far end of the room, above the dais where the music was being played. It was a violin sonata, and I was immediately held, not so much by the music as by the image which came into my mind as I gazed at the woman playing the violin. Her slender body was like a stem on which nodded, to the rhythm of the music, a strange exotic flower. The corolla of this flower was a human face, very white beneath an arch of raven

41

black hair, and it seemed to brood over the coiled tawny petals of the instrument, preserving an essential stillness in the midst of the force that agitated them. The notes of the piano, to whose rise and fall it seemed bound in some inevitable way, might have been the voice of a stream urging its way past the resisting stem of the flower that swayed above its swift current.

All my early fascination for this instrument, awakened long before by Fiddler Dick and long dormant, awoke again at this moment with a glow in which there was no longer any sense of aspiration or self-directed interest, a fire of renunciation and surrender. Once more an early impulse had found its fulfilment, its transformation, to become a conscious interest in my life.

13

Death

These scenes of childhood end abruptly with the death of my father. In the winter of my ninth year, he was taken ill with a fever; and the house became muted and silent. Mrs. Walker, the nurse from one of the cottages by Peacock's farm, whom I have not mentioned before, but who had attended my mother in all her confinements, was called in; and our cousin the doctor came from Kirby daily. He and my father were fast friends, and when the illness became critical, all his energies were devoted to the saving of this precious life. But in vain. Rheumatic fever developed. The air of anguish in every one, my mother's tearful eyes—these were obvious even to us children. One day leeches were brought, and stood in a glass jar on a shelf in the dairy. They were black, blind and sinister. But then we were taken away. I went to Howkeld, and one night I suffered intolerable earache, so that I cried aloud, and was poulticed with onions. The pain had gone in the morning, but by my aunt's tears I knew that my father was dead. The next day I was driven back to the Farm. The blinds were drawn, everywhere it was very still, and dark. We were taken upstairs to say good-bye to my dead father. The cold wintry light came evenly through the open slats of the venetian blind. My father lay on the bed, sleeping, as he always did, with his arms on the coverlet, straight down each side of his body. His beautiful face was very white, except for the red marks on his temples, where the leeches had clung. I was told to kiss that face; it was deadly cold, like the face of Little Meg's mother.

I felt stunned, but could not comprehend my loss, nor the grief of those about me. I moved away in the unnatural stillness, walking in a living sleep. Downstairs candles were burning on a table laden with cold meat and cakes. Then we all drove to Kirkdale, slowly over the frozen flint roads, and there a grave was ready dug at the east end of the Church, by the side of Mariana's. The dark cirque of fir-trees rose in the background, sighing in the frosty wind. The bell in the grey tower clanged its toneless note. The horses were not unyoked. Six friends of my father carried his coffin into the ancient church, and then to the grave. The earth fell with a hollow sound on to the lowered coffin. My mother sobbed against my uncle's shoulder. The last amen was murmured in that immemorial stillness, and when we had taken a last look at the forlorn coffin, we drove back swiftly over the frozen flint roads, horse-hooves beating clearly in the metallic air.

A few weeks later the sheep were driven into pens, the cattle labelled, and a crowd of farmers from far and near assembled at the Farm. A wagon was drawn out on the Green, to serve as a platform for the auctioneer. Everything was sold, except a few pieces of old furniture which my mother was fond of—even the books from the attic, the sermons tied in bundles, and the two volumes of the *Illustrated London News*. *Little Meg*, *Little Arthur*, *Evenings at Home*, and *Forget-me-not* alone were left for me.

We went to stay with a cousin at the other end of the Vale, but only for a few months. Then the elder of my two brothers and I left for a boarding-school, far away from these scenes; my childhood, the first phase of my life, was isolated: it grew detached in my memory and floated away like a leaf on a stream. But it never finally disappeared, as these pages witness. Instead, as this body of mine passes through the rays of experience, it meets bright points of ecstasy which come from the heart of this lost realm. But the realm is never wholly lost: it is reconstructed stage by stage whenever the sensibility recovers its first innocence, whenever eye and ear and touch and tongue and quivering nostril revive sensation in all its child-godly passivity.

To-day I found a withered stem of honesty, and shelled the pods between my thumb and finger; silver pennies, which grew between the fragrant currant-bushes. Their glistening surfaces, seeded, the very faint rustle they make in the wind—these sensations come direct to me from a moment thirty years ago. As they expand in my mind, they carry everything in their widening circle—the low crisp box-hedge which would be at my feet, the pear-trees on the wall behind me, the potato-flowers on the patch beyond the bushes, the ivy-clad privy at the end of the path, the cow pasture, the fairy rings—everything shimmers for a second on the expanding rim of my memory. The farthest tremor of this perturbation is lost only at the finest edge where sensation passes beyond the confines of experience; for memory is a flower which only opens fully in the kingdom of Heaven, where the eye is eternally innocent.

CHILDHOOD

The old elmtrees flock round the tiled farmstead; their silver-bellied leaves dance in the wind. Beneath their shade, in the corner of the Green, is a pond. In Winter it is full of water, green with weeds: in Spring a lily will open there.

The ducks waddle in the mud and sail in circles round the pond, or preen their feathers on the bank.

But in Summer the pond is dry, and its bed is glossy and baked by the sun, a beautiful soft colour like the skins of the moles they catch and crucify on the stable doors.

On the green the fowls pick grains, or chatter and fight. Their yellows, whites and browns, the metallic lustre of their darker feathers, and the crimson splash of their combs make an ever-changing pattern on the grass.

They drink with spasmodic upreaching necks by the side of the well.

PASTURELANDS

We scurry over the pastures
chasing the windstrewn oak-leaves.

We kiss
the fresh petals of cowslips and primroses.

We discover frog-spawn in the wet ditch.

THE POND

Shrill green weeds
float on the black pond.

A rising fish
ripples the still water

And disturbs my soul.

APRIL

To the fresh wet fields
and the white
froth of flowers

Came the wild errant
swallows with a scream.

THE ORCHARD

Grotesque patterns of blue-gray mould
cling to my barren apple-trees:
But in spring
pale blossoms break like flames
along black wavering twigs:
And soon
rains wash the cold frail petals
downfalling like tremulous flakes
even within my heart.

MOON'S FARM

A Dialogue for Three Voices

A cave in the old quarry
a dry ditch and a tumbledown barn
such is all my shelter.
The black-faced sheep have gone
and with them the shepherds . . .
That was twenty winters ago.
Then came the men with axes
cut down the spinneys and plantations
lopped off the branches
    and carted the timber away
leaving this desolation
    at the head of the dale.

Oh, I can nestle in a ferny glen
or in the rafters of a fallen roof
    in myrtle bushes at the edge of the bog
But I grow weak
    I have no nourishment
        I languish like a mist at noon.

Once it was different.
That was in the time of the holy men
monks who came over the moor
    from the abbey by the sea
to build a monastery in the slender woods
    at the dale's mouth.
Their path
led up the dale and across the hills
and on the hills they had many sheep
and cattle in the meadows below the hills

They dammed up the beck
  to make fishponds
and ran off a sluice
  to drive the millwheel.

They cared for me
and built me in with woods and garths
  with farmsteads and sheepfolds
    with chapels and graveyards
even their dead
  they gave to me.
Now the broken stones of their buildings
  lie under these grassy mounds and heather
I am left
  with birds and beetles for company
    and the little grey snails in the turf
Even the foxes and badgers
  have left this place
There is no strength at all
  left in the place.

About here it must have been
  but there is nothing left
    nothing left of Moon's Farm.
There was a clump of pines
  the last trees before the heather began
And a stone trough
  to gather the clear water from a rill
It fell from a stone spout which must have been very old
  fifty years ago they had given up carving such things
    from the solid stone
    (took too much time, they said)
Time, time
  folk were already beginning to be aware of time
    even then.

Not aware enough!
When you live all the time in the same place
Then you become aware of time.

SECOND VOICE

I begin to remember everything
    but how it has changed!
There were woods on the other side of the dale
    and down there
        by the beck
was Moon's Farm.
Not a stone or stick of it left!
That's a mystery—
    how completely a solid structure
        like a farmhouse
can vanish in fifty years!
The stones they would carry off
    to make a new road
        miles away
But what happened to the trees?
    there was even a stunted orchard
All gone.
All signs of human habitation
rubbed off the landscape.
And yet
    there is still something. I still feel
        the spirit of the place.

FIRST VOICE

He is becoming aware of me.

SECOND VOICE

It was made up of so many things:
the shapes of these hills
    and the changing shadows

the cries of birds
and the lapping of the stream over pebbles.
But more than that—
a sense of glory and yes
a sense of grief.
Glory in the present moment
Grief because it was all so momentary
so fleeting
so elusive.
And yet I am sure
it was more than an illusion
some spirit did inhabit these hills
some very ancient spirit.
The Roman legions passed this way
the stones of their roads lie under the heather
Did they salute her as they passed?
But there you are
already personifying the thing
imagining some wispy female.
The Romans were not so sentimental
their genius loci was masculine
the devil of a fellow.
Hullo!
there's someone coming up from the beck
looks like an old beggar woman
but what would she find up here?
She must have seen me from the other side
and now comes to investigate.
But she takes her time.

FIRST VOICE

Now he has seen me.
He is walking into my world with his innocent eyes
He is looking straight into my hiding-place.

SECOND VOICE

Good morning!
I did not expect to meet anybody up here. You surely
don't live hereabouts.

FIRST VOICE

Indeed I do. I have always
lived in this dale.

SECOND VOICE

Then perhaps you can help me. I too
used to live in this dale
but farther down.
I left fifty years ago
as a boy of ten
I went far away
into another country.
Today, for the first time
I have come back.
I find everything changed.

FIRST VOICE

Oh yes: it has changed a lot
in that long time.

SECOND VOICE

It is partly an illusion
or *was* an illusion.
You see: everything, yes, every thing
is much smaller than I can remember.
My childish eyes
had magnified everything
and now the world seems to have shrunk.

FIRST VOICE

When your possessions are small
  you enlarge them with wonder.
My world
  remains always the same

SECOND VOICE

You speak like an educated woman
  yet you say
    you have never left the dale.

FIRST VOICE

I have never left the dale: my schooling
  was indeed simple.

SECOND VOICE

But apparently profound.
I went to many schools
  and was no wiser in the end.
I did not know, for example,
  that this dale would shrink.
I thought I should find it
  as I had left it
    the people changed, of course
      most of them dead
        many gone away
but I thought the place would be the same.

FIRST VOICE

It changes slowly.
The trees are felled
  or brought down in a storm
and no one plants new ones.

The roofs fall in
  the stones crumble
    men go away in search of easier work.
Only the hills
  remain
    in their old shape.

SECOND VOICE

And why have you been left behind
apparently alone?

FIRST VOICE

I am not alone.
I have a Father.

SECOND VOICE

A Father! And how old is he?

FIRST VOICE

You must ask him—I don't know.

SECOND VOICE

Is he about?

FIRST VOICE

Yes: he is always about.
You will see him presently.

SECOND VOICE

Good! Are there any more in the family?

FIRST VOICE

That depends
  on what you mean by a family.
Sometimes
  we have people to stay with us.

SECOND VOICE

For a holiday, no doubt.

FIRST VOICE

From time to time.

SECOND VOICE

Now I can see your Father
  he is coming down the hillside.
But the sun is in his eyes
  he does not see us.

FIRST VOICE

Oh yes: he sees everything
he can stare the sun out
he can see in the dark.

SECOND VOICE

How extraordinary! You mean . . .

FIRST VOICE

Hush! About such things
  he must tell you himself.

THIRD VOICE

Ah! I thought I would catch up with you here.

SECOND VOICE

But I came
   from the opposite direction.

THIRD VOICE

Yes: but I came to meet you.

SECOND VOICE

But I don't understand . . .

THIRD VOICE

Never mind! The point is
What are you going to do next?

FIRST VOICE

He means
Where are you going to next?

SECOND VOICE

Does it matter to you?
I am not trespassing, am I?

FIRST VOICE

You are not trespassing
If you stay here.

THIRD VOICE

You surely have time enough.

SECOND VOICE

You mean
you would like me to stay with you?

FIRST AND THIRD VOICES

For as long as you like.

FIRST VOICE

You would gradually recover
the feeling of the place.

THIRD VOICE

You would gradually recover
the sense of the past.

SECOND VOICE

Ah, that's just what I came for.
I will gladly stay. I have the few necessary things
in that rucksack.

FIRST VOICE

I will go to prepare a bed for you.
I am afraid it will be a very simple one
we have no house.

SECOND VOICE

It is very kind of you
anything will do.

THIRD VOICE

We are what you would call tramps.

SECOND VOICE

Yes: but I don't see
what you can possibly find to live on
in a place like this.

THIRD VOICE

One needs less and less
after a certain age.

SECOND VOICE

Yes: that is what I am beginning to discover.

THIRD VOICE

Until one needs nothing at all.

SECOND VOICE

You mean
we die.

THIRD VOICE

That's right
you will die.

SECOND VOICE

Tell me: were you too
  here fifty years ago?

THIRD VOICE

Yes, of course.

SECOND VOICE

You don't remember me, I suppose?

THIRD VOICE

I remember you perfectly well
  the boy at the Scarlets.

SECOND VOICE

Yes: that was the name of our farm.
But surely
you cannot recognize in my wasted features
  the boy of fifty years ago?

THIRD VOICE

There are some things that do not change
  the shape of the skull
  the cadence of the voice.

SECOND VOICE

But if you remember me so well
why don't I remember you?
I would say
  I had never seen you before.

THIRD VOICE

No: in those days
    you were not aware of me.

SECOND VOICE

So we might say
you have the advantage over me.

THIRD VOICE

So we might say. But you will not forget me
ever again.

SECOND VOICE

It's not likely. Meeting you like this
    in this lonely place.
Can you tell me what the time is?
    it must be getting late . . .

                                        (*A shrill scream*)

What was that?

THIRD VOICE

A rabbit—perhaps, if we are lucky, a hare.
It is all we have to live on
    up here.

SECOND VOICE

I have heard wounded men scream like that.
But I was asking you the time . . .

THIRD VOICE

I can still see you
  the day you nearly lost your life
    in the mill-dam.

SECOND VOICE

You were there!

THIRD VOICE

Yes: standing on the far bank
  watching the water-rats
I saw how you were pulled out
  as good as dead.

SECOND VOICE

No wonder I didn't see you!
And shortly after that narrow squeak
  I went away.
That is why there was never any chance
  of getting to know you.
You stayed in the dale
  I never came back
    until today.

THIRD VOICE

I stayed here.

SECOND VOICE

And perhaps that was wise of you. I wonder
I wonder what I would have done
  had I stayed here
what would I have become.

THIRD VOICE

We can only become what we are.

SECOND VOICE

True enough—'Become what thou art!'—an oracle
I have always believed in.

THIRD VOICE

So it made no difference
    going away?

SECOND VOICE

No essential difference, I suppose. And yet
    it is said we only learn by experience.

THIRD VOICE

And what did experience teach you?

SECOND VOICE

To discover myself
    perhaps only that.

THIRD VOICE

And other people?

SECOND VOICE

They remained mysteries
    except in so far as I got
        inside their skulls
And even then
    it was pretty dark inside.

But how did you discover yourself?

Curiously enough
  in exploring other people.
I didn't discover that I was a male
  until I had known a female
I did not discover that I was an Englishman
  until I fought with a German
I did not discover that I was a European
  until I had lived in America.
Shall I go on?

Yes: to the end.

It has no end—yet.
I did not discover that I was alone in the world
  until I joined an army
I did not discover that I was brave
  until I had sheltered in a ditch with a coward
I did not discover that I was a liar
  until I met a man who never lied
    even to save his pride
I did not discover that I was sober
  until one night I got dead drunk
I did not discover that I could hate
  until I fell in love.
A mass of contradictions
  you will say.

THIRD VOICE

There is no unity in human character
Only God and the Devil are consistent.
But go on.

SECOND VOICE

I did not discover that I was a peasant
    until I became a poet
I did not discover that I was miserly
    until I became rich
I did not discover that I was strong
    until God had forsaken me.

THIRD VOICE

Until you had forsaken God.

SECOND VOICE

No: it did not happen like that
I did not deliberately forsake God.
Rather I clung to Him
    like a child to its mother's skirts.
But the garment was whisked away
    I fell to the ground.

THIRD VOICE

It may have been
God wanted you to stand alone.

SECOND VOICE

Alone? I have been alone
    all these years.

At first I was proud to be alone
I found I could stand without a hand
    clutching at the finger of God
I was defiant and cried: God is dead.
But then
    I grew less certain
It was not that I believed in a resurrection of the dead God.
But it became obvious
    that for some people he was still alive.
I could not convince them that he was dead
    and when they looked at me
        it was with eyes of pity
            as for someone who had lost á father or a son.
I scorned their pity
    but I no longer despised their belief.

You did not try
    to find your lost God?

No. If God is still alive
    he is with us now
staring us in the face
His face is the sky
His eyes are red berries in yon hedge
    or the glittering quartz in this stone.
His voice is that bird
    crying in the gorse bush
    or the water
        lapping over the pebbles in the beck.
If God exists
    he must be both immanent and ubiquitous
What sort of God would play hide-and-seek?

THIRD VOICE

It takes two to play such a game.

SECOND VOICE

Yes: man is just as necessary to God
    as God to man.
God depends for his existence
    on our recognition of Him.
God is reborn
    in every woman's womb.

THIRD VOICE

God exists but for a moment.

SECOND VOICE

The moment of our attention—or do you mean
that time will still exist
    when God is dead?

THIRD VOICE

That is what I mean.

SECOND VOICE

You are a very strange old man
    to talk so confidently
        about God and Fate.
I did not expect to find a man like you
    in such a lonely place.

In such a lonely place
no man would stay
who had not made his peace
    with the eyes in the berries
    and the voice in the beck.

SECOND VOICE

Yes: most of us ignore them
    run away from them
        and think we have escaped
            their obstinate questionings.
Oh, I too ran away from them
    and have managed fairly well to forget them!
And that is how we begin to deceive ourselves
that, at any rate, is how I
    began to deceive myself
        began to 'avoid the issue' as we say . . .
Avoid the issue!
To be honest I ought to say
        that that is how I began to practise hypocrisy . . .
Hypocrisy
    is perhaps rather a strong word for it
Let me call it dissimulation
I had a habit
    no, not a habit—an innate disposition
to identify myself with the other person.
Sometimes it worked
    and sometimes it didn't.
I could not identify myself with very poor people
    nor with very rich people
        their upbringings had been so different.
But if a Christian began to talk to me
    assuming that I was a Christian
        I did not disabuse him

or if an aggressive patriot began to talk to me
   assuming that I would be willing to destroy a whole city
     with a single bomb
again I did not disabuse him.
It was not cowardice—on some other occasion
I would freely express
   an unorthodox opinion.
It may sometimes have been indolence—what I call
   my lazy larynx
     (for I have always felt
       the effort of talking).
Such is my physical disposition . . .
Voices
   how they expose us
     how they form our thoughts
A man's mind
   is an echo of his voice—or rather
     of his voices.

THIRD VOICE

Voices?

SECOND VOICE

Yes: we have two voices
   the instinctive voice that flows like water from a spring
     or blood from a wound
   and the intellectual voice that blares like a fanfare
     from some centre in the brain.

THIRD VOICE

I have only one voice
   but it is new every day.

Like the sun. But the ancient man who said
   that the sun was new every day
had spent his life seeking himself.
But the same ancient man said
   that though you travel in every direction
     you will never find the boundaries of the self
      so deep is the logos of it.
And that is the truth I have discovered. In the end
   I came back here
     to the scene of my birth and infancy.
I thought I might find the truth about myself here
but I don't see the end of my search yet!
So deep is the logos!

THIRD VOICE

The logos? Now that
   is not a word we use here.

SECOND VOICE

If I could tell you what such a word means
   I should be at the end of my task!
It is the most mysterious word
   in the history of human thought.
'In the beginning was the Word
   and the Word was with God
     and the Word was God'. . .
I began to puzzle over that sentence
   when I was still a child
and I think most Christians have wondered
   why such a strange ambiguous word
     Word itself
should stand at the beginning of their Gospel.
Perhaps it is because the word

is the only link that exists between the known and the
                                              unknown
   between man and the cosmos.
If man had not been able to utter the word of God
   he would never have conceived the idea of God
And so God was first manifested to man in speech
   and in the poetry inherent in speech
      in the logos.
That is perhaps fairly obvious
but the more I have pondered on this fact
   the more I have realized the predicament into which we
      as men
   are thrown by this dependence on logos.
For two things could happen
   and did happen.
In the beginning there was the cosmos
   (or nature as we more politely call it)
and in the midst of the cosmos
   and part of it
      was man
         growing aware of his environment.
He slowly perfected words to express his predicament.
But then the word became God
the instrument that had enabled man to express the idea of
                                         an outer cosmos
   was identified with the idea to be expressed.
Men then worshipped
   not the cosmos of which they were a part
      but the idea of the cosmos which they could
                        separate from themselves as a word
and make absolute as an idea.
But that was not the end.
Eventually
   and not so long ago
man conceived the notion that his kind
in inventing the word
   the logos
had invented God.

The idea of God
   had not risen from man's experience of the world
   but had been an original intuition of the mind
   an idea divinely inspired
     a glimpse of some transcendental realm of being
where time does not exist.

THIRD VOICE

I cannot conceive of such a realm.

SECOND VOICE

Nor I.
I have always felt perfectly satisfied
   with a natural outlook on life.
By this I do not mean
   the outlook of what is called natural science.
Materialists of that kind
   stand this side of the logos.
They assume
   that their words and signs are fixed and measurable
                             entities
   that with their words and signs
     they can explain the cosmos.
That is childish
   or perverse.
But it is merely a higher childishness
   to go to the opposite extreme
     that is to say
       beyond the natural function of the logos
to assume the autonomous reality
   of a realm with which we cannot communicate
     except by means of the logos.
In the beginning was the word
   and in the end are many words
     nets to catch the butterfly truth.

THIRD VOICE

Truth! so that is what you are looking for!
You thought you would find the truth up here?

SECOND VOICE

I'm sorry—truth
is a word I did not mean to bring into our conversation
    it is an evil word I have sworn not to use.
Truth
    is that for which men kill each other.
I limit my search to myself
I know that my self is different from all other selves
    and that what I discover
        is not going to be the envy of anyone else.

THIRD VOICE

But if you discover the truth
    you will be the envy of the world.
You must therefore avoid the truth
    even the truth about yourself.

SECOND VOICE

Well, if I do discover the truth about myself
I must keep it to myself.
    It will be my secret.

THIRD VOICE

What is the good of a secret
    known only to yourself?

Perhaps I should say
  the secret of my strength
   strength is the knowledge of one's limits
    and that knowledge
     helps a man to endure his fate.
The man that knows himself
  can almost foresee his fate.

THIRD VOICE

Is that any consolation?

SECOND VOICE

Consolation?—not exactly.
But it gives to life
  the excitement of a game of chance.
There a man goes
  spinning out the thread of his destiny
   millions more are doing the same thing.
The threads cross
  and turn
   and cross again
and the pattern that emerges we call history.
A crazy pattern
  but the only one that exists. . . .

THIRD VOICE

And when the thread is cut?

SECOND VOICE

Why, then the pattern changes
but so infinitely little
  it makes no difference.

THIRD VOICE

But the thread is your individual life:
it makes a difference to you.

SECOND VOICE

Not so long as I remain
aware of the beauty of the pattern.

THIRD VOICE

You are sitting on the edge of the moor.
Beyond the moor is the sea
    the unknown
We are standing on the edge of the world
    and what do we see
        as we look over the edge?

SECOND VOICE

Our human eyes see very little
    the stars and the planets
worlds beyond worlds
    universe without end.

THIRD VOICE

You don't know
    that it is without end.

SECOND VOICE

I know nothing
    beyond what my eyes
        or my eyes aided by clever instruments
tell me.
I can guess a little.

THIRD VOICE

Yes, but at the end of your guessing
  what do you see?

SECOND VOICE

Nothing
I cannot see anything beyond the evidence of my senses.
There may be something
  an unending Thing
  Nothing or Something
I do not know.

THIRD VOICE

And you do not fear
  anything?

SECOND VOICE

Fear? Why should I be afraid?

THIRD VOICE

You are not afraid of the unknown?

SECOND VOICE

I do not think the unknown is a subject
  to inspire one with feelings of any kind.
Before such an unconceivable concept
  my mind is merely blank.

THIRD VOICE

Blank?
Have you then no curiosity?

SECOND VOICE

Of course—unending, restless, curiosity.
But my curiosity
    nibbles away at the edge of the known
    it does not take a leap into nothingness.
It looks back at the wide and solid expanse of the known
    looks back
        and is lost in wonder.

THIRD VOICE

Wonder?

SECOND VOICE

That is another of my pet words. Wonder
    is the antidote to fear
    the essence of courage.
We say we are lost in wonder
    as though it were a forest
        or a sea.
But wonder invades us like the warmth of the sun.
Our very consciousness expands when we discover
    some corner of the pattern of the universe
        realize its endless implications
        and know ourselves
            to be part of that intricate design.

THIRD VOICE

But surely that discovery
    is the beginning of humility?

SECOND VOICE

No: humility is for human relationships
    an attitude of man to man.

But when I discover the same geometrical proportions
    in the human body and in a flower
        or a crystal
    in a cathedral
        and in a planetary system
then I am not humble.
Nor am I proud, for it is no effort of man
    that has created such correspondencies.
I am excited by such a thought
perhaps my heart beats more quickly
        or my eyes dilate
            for I am filled with wonder.

THIRD VOICE

But the day will come
    when your heart will stop beating
and your eyes will no longer
    be aware of any of these wonders.

SECOND VOICE

Yet death
    is the greatest wonder of all.
That life can be extinguished
    is a fact as wonderful as the fact
        that it can be conceived.
The chance that you or I
    or any particular person
is born
    is an infinite one
and with the thought of the infinitude of that chance
    we should be ready to accept
        the finiteness of death. It is
            simply
our fate.

You did not hear me return
   but I have been standing behind you
     listening.
Your bed is ready.

SECOND VOICE

Thank you: I will come along presently. You were kind
   to listen patiently to all this nonsense.

FIRST VOICE

I did not mean to interrupt
   but I thought you had finished.

THIRD VOICE

It was the word Fate
   that made us pensive.

SECOND VOICE

It is a word that seems to end all argument.
There is no appeal against fate
   and no sense in discussing it.

THIRD VOICE

Not if you imagine it as an enemy. But it isn't!
It has been said
   man's character is his fate.

FIRST VOICE

Man is more than his fate.
Man is moulded in a womb
   and dissolved in earth
His foundations are two tombs
He is like earth uprisen.

I think I agree. A character can be uprooted.
We are proud
  of our upright posture
  of our legs that can carry us out of this dale
    into the wide world.
Men are proud of the machines that carry them over the seas
  through the air.
But they carry their character with them
  and their character is their destiny.
But
  our characters are sometimes seduced.
If I am sitting in an aeroplane above the Atlantic
I have surrendered my fate to the pilot of the plane.
It might be said
  only a man of my character would fly across the Atlantic
but the same anonymous chances
  follow me on land and by sea.
It is not in man's character to desert his home—
That is what one calls
  tempting Fate
and tempting Fate does not mean
  that we act as if we accept our fate
it means acting in defiance of our fate.
I do not mean
  that restlessness cannot be our fate.
Man was once a nomadic animal
  and traces of the nomad
    linger in his groins.
But we have perfected ourselves in stillness.

FIRST VOICE

In suffering and in joy.

SECOND VOICE

Yes: I meant to imply suffering and joy.
Fate is not ameliorative.

But who can separate
    beauty and terror
        suffering and joy?
I remember a valley in Greece.
I came to it
    when the light was failing.
The rocky hills were purple
    the sky a thin icy green
        fading eastward to a slatey grey.
There was a huge mound, partly excavated
    to reveal colossal stones
        the foundations of a fortress.
In the hillside was a tomb
    the tomb of a legendary king
        faultlessly shaped and tense
        like the inside of an eggshell.
I viewed it by the light
    of a fire of withered thyme . . .
When I emerged
    it was dark in the valley and I felt around me
        the nameless terror that had penetrated the lives of that
                                                    ancient king
            his adulterous queen
                and all their melancholy issue.
Their fates had overtaken them
    in that place
        more than three thousand years ago
and man had not dared to build again
    not on such a site of horror.
But I knew then
    that man's fate is not like a seed
    carried hither and thither by the wind
not like spawn on a restless tide
But is the creation of generations of men
    men who have lived in one place
        and absorbed its mysteries.

Mysteries?

Perhaps there are no mysteries of time or place
but there are mysteries of life.
A mystery
 is what is hidden, and it is Life
 not God
  that loves to hide.
It is Life
 not God
  that is mysterious.
The Greeks were right again: it is Life
 that plays the game of hide-and-seek
The rhythm of the seasons
 is the interplay of Life and Death. In the person of
          Persephone
 it is Life itself
  that disappears for a wintry season.
But hiding involves a hiding-place. In Eleusis
 you can still see the pit
 down which Persephone sank
  to Pluto's dark realm.
All the ancient myths
 are precisely located. And today we have no myths
because we have no sense of place.
Our beliefs
 are like untethered balloons
 they drift into the clouds
  into the transcendental inane.
I would sooner men worshipped a tree or a rock.

And yourself
 what have you worshipped?

Ah! you have some right
   to ask me that question
      for it embarrasses me.
The truth is
   I have never been able to worship anything
      not even myself.
Worship is an act of adoration
   the complete surrender of the self to some Other
      to some Otherness.
It must be a great relief
   to get rid of that burden sometimes
      to feel utterly empty
         like a room that has been swept and made bright
            ready for a new occupant
to return to a body that has been renewed in ecstasy!
It is an illusion, of course
   but one of the desirable illusions.

FIRST VOICE

Have you then lived without illusions?

SECOND VOICE

Never for a moment.
I have lived with the illusion
   that I was in love
with the illusion
   that my loved ones loved me
with the illusion
   that I could give happiness to other people
      as you would give a rose to a young girl
with the illusion
   that other people would see the world with my eyes
      and love the things that I love

with the illusion
   that my words would open men's hearts
      and give them understanding.
For fifty years I have lived
   in successive states of illusion
      and I am still not completely
disillusioned.

THIRD VOICE

What illusions remain to you?

SECOND VOICE

The illusion that it is not yet too late
   for any of these illusions to be re-established.
The illusion
   that a voice in the wilderness echoes in some green valley
the illusion that the wind
   or a bird
will take up the seed I have scattered on stony ground
   and drop it in a fertile field
the illusion
   that bitterness is dissolved in the serenity of old age
the illusion
   that I shall die a happy man.

THIRD VOICE

And at the time of your death
what could make you happy?

SECOND VOICE

To die without fear and trembling.

THIRD VOICE

You are describing a state of happiness. You do not tell us
   what would ensure such a state.

SECOND VOICE

I am not sure that I know.
I suppose at the end I shall come to another Place
    it might be this dale-head
    it might be my white bedroom
    it might be a busy street.
I might die in pain
    in weariness
        or in despair.
But if at the last moment
I could see some perfect form
    it might be this fern at my feet
    or a sparrow flickering past my window
    or a painting on the wall
    or some poet's vision of eternity
        like a great Ring of pure and endless Light
        all calm, as it was bright . . .
Granted that I could at the last moment
see some bright image
    I should die without fear and trembling.
It is when we look into the abyss of nothingness
    infinite nothingness
that we lose courage
    and die swearing
        or die praying.

FIRST VOICE

Yes: men should hold on to tangible things.
Stay with me in these hills and glens
where the birds cry lovingly to their young
    and the waters are never silent.

THIRD VOICE

Die to the day and its trivialities
Die to the sense of time.

FIRST VOICE

Or to the sense of place
to the place of generation and birth.

THIRD VOICE

Live with the sun by day and with the stars by night.

FIRST VOICE

Live with your eyes and ears
    and the exercise of your subtle fingers.

THIRD VOICE

Live in the moment of attention.

FIRST VOICE

Live in the presence of things.

                                        (*A silence*)

SECOND VOICE

It is getting dark.
I can hardly see you.

FIRST VOICE

Yes: it is dark now.
I shall lead you to your bed.

SECOND VOICE

You said it was down by the beck, didn't you?

FIRST VOICE

It is not far.

THIRD VOICE

And the way up and the way down are the same.
I go up the hill.

FIRST VOICE

My Father will be with us again tomorrow.

SECOND VOICE

As boys we used to come here
 to gather wild daffodils.
At Moon's Farm the pump was in the kitchen
 a well of clean crystal water.
And there was an old clock
 standing opposite the kitchen door.
It had a robin
 or perhaps it was a wren
painted on its white face
 but the fingers never moved
It was always 12.25 at Moon's Farm.
12.25 is God's time.

THE IVY AND THE ASH

The ivy and the ash
cast a dark arm
across the beck.
In this rocky ghyll
I sit and watch
the eye-iris water move
like muscles over stones
smooth'd by this ageless action.

The water brings
from the high fell
an icy current of air.
There is no sun to splinter
the grey visionary quartz.
The heart is cool
and adamant among the rocks
mottled with wet moss.

Descend into the valley
explore the plain
even the salt sea
but keep the heart
cool in the memory
of ivy, ash
and the glistening beck
running swiftly through the black rocks.

SONNET

One day you will intuitively come
Home again driving westward
Into the burning sun: memory
a dusty screen that blinds the vision
You will wind through the narrow lanes
Over the frequent culverts where willows
Sprout in clumps. The marshes
Remember the marigolds and over the farm
The pines stretch agonised arms
It will be still and you will descend
Into an arena of yellow corn
That not a breath of wind stirs

And a rook if it should swerve in the sky
Will move the whole world momentously.

EXILE'S LAMENT

Here where I labour hour by hour
The folk are mean and land is sour.

God grant I may return to die
Between the Riccall and the Rye.

A Dearth of Wild Flowers

I

Under the Hill

More than forty years passed before I could return to the scenes of my childhood. I then found a house—Sterne would have called it a 'philosophical cottage', but it is about twice the size of Shandy Hall—situated two and a half miles to the south-east of the Farm, on the other side of that long ridge from which the windows of Stamper's Farm had once sent out their flashing signals. This ridge, known as Cauklass Bank, lies like a great green caterpillar in the basin of the Vale, and along its top runs a wide track, some three miles long. The caterpillar eats its way towards Gilling Gap and Coxwold in the west, as if trying to escape from the basin, its tail still trailing in Ness, a hamlet where as a child I had bought my 'goodies'. But, alas, the sweet shop has gone, with much else from memory's bright inventory.

To reach Stonegrave from the Farm you must pass through the village of Nunnington, where I received my first schooling, and then ascend an ancient avenue of limes and sycamores, nearly half a mile in length. On reaching the top of the bank (as hills are called here), you will suddenly seem to be at the still centre of the world. Cauklass (the name being a corruption of caulk leys, or chalk lands), is a hill 'celebrated both for the salubrity of its air, and the beautiful views which it commands'. So wrote the Reverend Thomas Alexander Browne, curate of Nunnington, in 1824, and his further description of this place, to become my familiar haunt, must be quoted:

'The surface, before the inclosure took place, was covered with a strong bent, a kind of short, coarse, elastic grass, similar to that on the training ground, Hambleton, and being a mile or more in extent was formerly used, occasionally, for a similar purpose; and at some distant period, as appears from the old map and plan, was a race-course; at the western extremity of which, near Stonegrave, was erected a stand. This course has run parallel to, if not in the very line of, the present avenue of aged firs, which crowns the summit of the hill, and forms so conspicuous an object, in whatever direction it is approached.'*

Browne continues his enthusiastic description of Cauklass, which, he says, being situated between two lovely vales and commanding one of the most beautiful and extensive prospects in the neighbourhood, need not shrink from a comparison with the artificial beauties of the grounds at Castle Howard, Gilling and Duncombe Park. 'From hence,' he boasts, 'on a clear day, may be seen distinctly no less than twenty-two towns, villages, and hamlets, and sixteen churches . . . These views are noticed in the third Canto of Mrs. Dunlop's poem, entitled Edmund of Ryedale. . . .'

Stonegrave, to which I came in September 1949, is situated on the steeper southern slope of Cauklass—a small but neat village, says Browne, 'so completely hid in approaching it from the north, that the traveller stands on the very precipice that immediately overlooks it, before he is aware of its presence. Here, sheltered from the northern blast, and, as it were nestling, and seeking protection under its friendly bank, may each inhabitant feelingly acknowledge the truth and beauty of those celebrated lines of Goldsmith:

> *Dear is that home to which his soul conforms,*
> *And dear that hill which shields him from the storms,*
> *And as a child, when scaring sounds molest,*
> *Clings close and closer to his mother's breast,*
> *So the loud tempest, and the whirlwind's roar,*
> *But bind him to his native mountain more.'*

* *Historia Rievallensis: containing the history of Kirkby Moorside, and an account of the most important places in its vicinity; together with brief notices of the more remote or less important ones. To which is prefixed a dissertation on the animal remains and other curious phenomena, in the recently discovered cave at Kirkdale.* By the Rev. W. Eastmead, author of *Observations on Human Life,* and Honorary Member of the Yorkshire, Hull, and Whitby, Literary and Philosophical Societies. London and York, 1824.

The Rev. Thomas Alexander Browne contributed to this volume the articles on Nunnington, Stonegrave, Oswaldkirk, Gilling, and Slingsby.

In Domesday Stonegrave is spelt *Stanegrif,* or *Steingrif,* and there are several other variations in ancient documents, all of which show that the termination (like those of other places such as Mulgrave and Walsgrave) comes from the Saxon word *griff,* which Young, in his *History of Whitby,* defines as 'a dingle, or narrow valley, with a rocky fissure-like chasm at the bottom'. This is rather too extreme as a description of the site of Stonegrave, but the road that passes through the village is steep, and on its northern side is a vertical cliff, against which some of the cottages are built.

Apart from the church and the rectory, the village now consists of three farmsteads and fourteen cottages, with a total of about sixty inhabitants. A hundred years ago it was considerably larger —some houses have disappeared and those that remain are not so densely populated as they must have been in 1824—Browne relates the 'singular and amazing fact, that the late rector of Stonegrave, and his parish clerk, had the unusual number of fifteen children each; a singular and remarkable coincidence, which can scarcely be paralleled in the annals of any other parish in the kingdom'. In our own time no family has exceeded a third of that number, and one or two of the cottages are occupied by single people. The parish records show that in 1743 there were about 40 families in the parish; in 1764 33 families. In 1831 the population was 189; by 1881 it had sunk to 140, and in 1900 to 127 (26 houses). In 1931 the parish boundaries were redrawn, which probably accounts for the further drastic reduction in the number of inhabitants.

The shrinking population, apart from any decline in the Christian faith, led to a uniting of the benefices of Stonegrave and Nunnington in 1946. But the Stonegrave rectory had been abandoned as a rectory some fourteen years earlier and sold (with protests from the indignant ghosts of former rectors) to a Roman Catholic family, who had the tithe-barn, which had also served sometimes as a school, consecrated as a chapel. They repaired the house, but after a few years left it, and it was the second of its secular owners who sold it to me in 1949.

I must have been there as a child—I vaguely remember a tea-party on the lawn—and since the school at Nunnington served also this village, I must have known boys from Stonegrave. The house is about thirty-eight paces in length, with two shorter wings projecting to the north. This northern aspect is regular and even severe, but as soon as one emerges on the southern side it presents a very different face, long and even in elevation, but broken by twenty windows irregular in design and spacing. It is built of honey-coloured stone and roofed with the warm crimson pantiles characteristic of all the old houses in Ryedale.

We know almost exactly when it was built, or rebuilt, for it was a rector called James Worsley, appointed to the living in 1747, who had this done, presumably soon after his induction. That a rectory existed on the site before this is certain—parts of the present structure are earlier than 1747 and indeed there is ghostly evidence of two or three houses: the 'two wings towards the Town street', as they are called in a terrier of 1786, had then been recently added. But in the main the building is 'Queen Anne' in style, though 'Georgian' by date. It was erected of local stone by local masons, and differs little (save in size) from the nearby farm-houses of the same period. As the word indicates, as a 'rectory' it had since the Reformation been in the King's books, and in 1824 its value for taxation was £23 6s. 8d.

These details are perhaps of no great interest to the common reader, and my own concern is not with history or topography, but with personal and spiritual associations. It is sufficient to say that once I had seen (or revisited) the place, which was in the summer of 1948, my heart was set on possessing it; and though the negotiations were more prolonged than might have been anticipated, I did finally secure possession, and made such arrangements of my work and social obligations that I was able to live for at least half the days of the year in a house some 215 miles from London.

The village is small—but for the church it would be called a hamlet. It once had an inn, which to my delight I discovered was called 'The Wings of Liberty'. Small as the village is, its church has a recorded history that goes back to the eighth century. In 757 it is mentioned in a letter from Pope Paul I to Eadbert, King of Northumbria, in which the king is ordered, as he values his salvation, to restore the monasteries at Stonegrave, Coxwold and Jarrow to their rightful owners. Such a monastery was probably an outlying missionary post from Whitby where an abbey for monks and nuns had been founded by Oswy, king of Northumbria, in 658, in celebration of his victory over Penda, king of

Mercia. Saint Hilda was its first abbess, and the poet Caedmon, the earliest English Christian poet 'who sang the beginning of created things', became a monk there in Hilda's time. The Saxon cross now in the church is all that survives from the period before the Norman Conquest, and it may be a remnant of this first monastery.

This church dedicated to the Holy Trinity once had a wall-painting of 'Sta Maria Salome', and a chapel dedicated to Saint Lawrence. The twelfth-century arches are noble, and on the north side have alternate courses of light and dark stones, as in Durham Cathedral. There are two small but fine corbels, carved with stylized animal heads in the Hiberno-Saxon style, and round one of the scalloped capitals is a band of ornamental medallions in the Byzantine style; one of them depicts a mermaid upside down. The carver must have been interrupted in his work, for the series breaks off with an uncompleted design. There is much fine woodwork in the church, including a screen dated 1637, but all this and much else was displaced and reconstituted in the necessary but disastrous restoration of the church, which took place in 1862. Scraped and dressed, re-roofed and redeemed, it stands like the village church everywhere, a monument to an age of faith and a melancholy reminder of crafts now defunct.

The sense of the past invests the whole village, the church, and the house in which I now live. To succumb to this sense is sentimental, and can be destructive of a proper sense of the present, of reality. I, who cannot be accused of having no sense of the present —or indeed, of the future: have I not been identified with 'the Demon of Progress'?—indulge the sense of the past only by instinct, by some unconscious craving for equanimity, for compensation. In other countries—in Sweden, in Brazil, in British Columbia—I have found houses that are the perfection of modern taste, visual expressions of the abstract harmony and grace that I admire in the art of the present. I have tried to imagine life in such crystal cabinets, but I have not had the desire or the will to achieve it. The art of living is in this respect like any other art—it must be spontaneous if it is to be deeply enjoyed. Only organic processes are spontaneous, and what the intellect plans, logically and coherently, is never organic. The dweller in a crystal cabinet must from time to time flee to the primeval forests of Africa or to the Cyclades to fill his sensibility with a wild contrast. But between these extremes lies the vast conglomeration of our industrial civilization—a wilderness so arid and offensive that no organic life is possible within its limits. This civilization will either destroy itself or transform itself—at present it seems bent on self-destruction. Meanwhile either we are imprisoned (by economic necessity, it will be said, but also by our psychological obsessions) or we escape—into artificial wildernesses. A house in the country is not the only artificial wilderness: there are, if we can afford them, yachts and caravans, or, if we have a vocation, monasteries and colleges. Country houses are miniature monasteries, not perhaps much larger than Whitby in Saint Hilda's time; completely anachronistic, hated by the bureaucratic taxmen, resented even by the industrialized farmer, islands of green comfort in a land that slowly but inevitably lies fallow to the tractor and the bulldozer. In the last ten years I have seen more than one beautiful country house razed to the ground, every stone and beam vanish, to be replaced by a timber-yard or a bacon-factory. There are still a sufficient number of quixotic Englishmen who will deny themselves all other pleasures so that they may for a few years live in these green oasic mansions; but it is not for long. The past has vanished and we are the last outposts of a civilization in retreat.

2

Kin to the Stone

This was a phrase used by one of the last of the moorland masons, to explain his addiction to a craft in which his sons would not follow him: he could not change because he and his like were 'kin to the stone'. Stone differs from brick and other building materials in that it is used in its natural state, quarried from the earth itself and 'dressed' by hand. Only wood can compete in naturalness, but it perishes too quickly if exposed, and easily catches fire. I have seen beautiful wooden houses in Western Canada and in Scandinavia, but they feel too impermanent, cabins for a brief stay on this earth. Wooden architecture has no visible history. As for bricks: the Egyptians and Assyrians made them because stones were so rare that they had to be reserved for the construction of temples and the carving of sacred images. Brick, in stone country like Yorkshire, Cumberland or the Cotswolds, is a shoddy intrusion.

I am stating a prejudice, for I must admit that when compelled to make the best of this material, as in Amsterdam and some of the cities of northern Germany, brick can be gracious and colourful: a pinchbeck substitute for golden stone, but still a matter of art. But it gives me no pleasure as a sheltering substance, as a shell within which to live and have my being. Always at home in stone country, I am vaguely ill at ease within a cold oven of baked bricks.

The landscape round Stonegrave is pocked with small quarries from which people have taken the stone to build their houses and churches. The modern quarry with its machinery is often an ugly scar on the hillside, but the old quarries were soon covered with undergrowth; bramble and hazel, and sometimes conifers find sufficient substance for root-hold. Most of the wild life that survives has found a refuge in these oases of the deserts made by the tractor.

The love of landscape must feed on intimacy as well as on magnitude: there must be a continual counterplay between the inscape of nature and its 'waking empire, wide as dreams'. Gerard Manley Hopkins, who invented the necessary word 'inscape', understood this perfectly, as perhaps only Traherne before him. In his Journal (May 9, 1871) there is a passage about bluebells which expresses this sense in utmost acuity: 'In the little wood opposite the light they stood in blackish spreads or sheddings like the spots on a snake. The heads are then like throngs and solemn in grain and grape-colour . . . The bluebells in your hand baffle you with their inscape, made to every sense: if you draw your fingers through them, they are lodged and struggle with the shock of wet heads; the long stalks rub and click and flatten to a fan on one another like [sic] your fingers themselves would when you passed the palms hard across one another, making a brittle rub and jostle like the noise of a hurdle strained by leaning against; then there is the faint honey smell and in the mouth the sweet gum when you bite them. But this is easy, it is the eye they baffle . . .'* There follows a minute description of the form of the bluebell, but my point has been made: the eye, in its near infinite range, must travel from the inscape of a flower, of a bird's feather, the rime on twigs or the skeleton of a leaf to the roll and rise, the imbricated nabs and scars of the distant moorland reaches. Mountains I have no love for; they are the accidents of nature, masses thrown up in volcanic agony. But moors and fells are moulded by gentle forces, by rain water and wind, and are human in their contours and proportions,† inducing affection rather than awe.

Nevertheless, the moors have sublimity, the sublimity Emily Brontë so beautifully celebrated. I shall speak about it in a later chapter, but here I am concerned with milder feelings. They begin

* *The Note-Books and Papers of Gerard Manley Hopkins.* Edited by Humphry House. Oxford, 1937, pages 145-6.

† Compare Wordsworth, *Topographical Description of the Country of the Lakes* (1820), conclusion:

'. . . a happy proportion of component parts is generally noticeable among the landscapes of the North of England; and, in this characteristic essential to a perfect picture, they surpass the scenes of Scotland, and, in a still greater degree, those of Switzerland.'

with the stone flags of the kitchen floor and passages of my house, each a pattern as beautiful as a painting by my friend Antonio Tapies; they extend to the external walls, abraded by rain and frost, sun-soaked and annealed to the hill behind the house. Each step in the garden, and beyond the macadamized scar of the public road, is like the shift of a slide in some magic lantern, revealing a new pattern of stones or grasses, of bark or leaves, bushes and gateposts, cart-tracks and hedges, till finally the eye lifts to the explosive splendour of the oaks and ashes, the beeches and elms. One immense poplar near my house, a cotton-wood if I am not mistaken, has all the calligraphic passion of a brush draw-ing by Sesshu. It is a Zen shrine to which I pay habitual homage, but already one large branch has fallen and it is a question whether the shrine will outlast its solitary worshipper.

I never exhaust the beauty of trees and woods. Careless of their species, I observe them as patterns against the sky, perhaps most beautiful when leafless. But though leafless they are never lifeless. The leaves are scarcely fallen when new buds begin shyly to press through the tender bark, like dark blebs of blood. There are three hundred and sixty-five days in a year and a tree has the same number of faces, or rather facets, for it is a composite picture of many minute changes.

Woods in this region are of every conceivable size and com-position, short of the forest. Forests we had, like the famous Galtres Forest that stretched from the Howardian Hills to the walls of York, which was one of the haunts of Robin Hood—a conical hill at the northern extremity, at the foot of Whitestone Cliff, is still known as Robin Hood's Outlook. But now the only forests are those planted by the Forestry Commission. Sentimental naturalists despise these mustered ranks of conifers, but I confess I love to wander along their geometrical glades. I love the dark needle-soft aisles, where only fungi grow, and a fox spreads his pungent trail.

Perhaps only once or twice a year there is a chance to wander in these woods when sunlight has succeeded hoar frost or a light fall of snow, and the whole scene scintillates in electric brilliance. Very rarely such an event takes place in April, when the first pale green leaves have already unfolded, and the undergrowth is starred with primroses and violets. I am then reminded of some-thing very unnatural but still poetic, those crystallized fruits we sometimes eat at Christmas; but these are clumsy compared with a frosted veil of snowflakes on a bed of violets.

One of the special joys in springtime is to wander along the banks of the Dove in Farndale. It is too far away to walk there from Stonegrave, so I leave the car in Low Mills some week-day (for alas, the sight is now so famous that thousands of people descend at week-ends from far and wide, so that we natives must turn 'wardens'). Here for miles along the banks of the beck blooms 'a crowd, a host, of golden daffodils'. Wordsworth's poem, and Dorothy's Journal,* are so familiar that it is impossible to feel the same ecstasy that William and his sister experienced when they were first surprised by the sight of wild daffodils growing in a long belt along the shore of Grasmere. I have no wish to claim some superior virtue for the daffodils of Farndale, but there is a difference. Dorothy's daffodils 'grew among the mossy stones about and about them; some rested their heads upon these stones as on a pillow for weariness; and the rest tossed and reeled and danced, and seemed as if they verily laughed with the wind, that blew upon them over the lake; they looked so gay, ever glancing, ever changing'. William heightened these effects in his poem though I feel that some of the words he used (he added them in 1815, eight years after the poem was first composed) words like 'twinkle', 'sprightly', 'jocund', take away from the perfect natural-ness of Dorothy's description. The daffodils in Farndale are not jocund, nor sprightly, for they are not agitated by a wind blowing directly over a lake. The Dove flows through the loveliest of all these dales, and meanders through the meadows, now cutting steeply into its banks, now darting into a little grove of willows. The daffodils bloom on the sandy peninsulas made by the meandering beck. They may sometimes rest their heads on a stone, but more often shelter against the mossy stump of a willow, or bunch in the gnarled veins of exposed tree-roots. They are shy and small, their compact heads steady on rather sturdy stalks, and though in the sunshine they seem from a distance like a golden overflow from the beck, they are perfectly indigenous, one with the willows and the primroses, part of an Eden that should remain forever undesecrated.

From a distance these green and flowery dales are invisible in

* *Journals of Dorothy Wordsworth.* Edited by E. de Selincourt. 2 vols. London, 1941. The Grasmere Journal (1802), 15th April.

the humped grandeur of the moors. The moors are one's natural love, the body to which trees and flowers, running becks and wooded dales, are but incidental, green wrinkles on an immense and ageless visage. The detail of a moor is as fascinating as any I know, but I admit its beauty is not easily transmitted. Apart from a few flowering grasses, some worts and celandines, the ground is densely thatched with heather, ling and bracken. Where a gill cuts into the slope, one may find rarer and more delicate ferns, but the overwhelming texture is rough and springy. The stems of a heather plant are metallic in their bronze or black glossiness, and with age aggregate into a dense network, against which the grouse shelter. The grass that grows in irregular patches between the clumps of heather is equally wiry, but the horned and black-faced moor-sheep find sustenance in it. These sheep are part of the landscape, self-subsisting in flocks that may number two or three hundred. They are rounded up and branded after lambing-time, but their numbers, and even their ownership, remain indefinite.

On the riggs or ridges of the moors are many howes, the barrows or burial mounds of the Celtic people who first inhabited this region in neolithic times. All of them have long since been excavated, mostly by amateurs about a hundred years ago. Canon Atkinson, in *Forty Years in a Moorland Parish*,* which was first published in 1891, confesses to the examination of between eighty and one hundred of them, and though most of the mounds had been tampered with before his time, 'a blank day was a thing we hardly knew'. On one occasion he carried home 'no less than eight sepulchral vessels of one kind or another; and one of them was found on examination to contain, over and above the usual complement of bones, a very beautiful and finely polished axe-hammer of fine-grained granite'. Atkinson considered himself a scientific antiquarian, and was indeed a very cultured clergyman, but he relates how on one occasion his spade 'suddenly passed through no less than four thicknesses of "Ancient British" pottery', whereas his 'energetic friend with his trenchant shovel shore off at one stroke one third part of a rather large cinerary vase'. This particular howe had been disturbed before Atkinson began his digging, but he was lucky enough to find 'in the very middle of this medley of burnt human bone and sherds . . . a small

* *Forty Years in a Moorland Parish.* By Rev. J. C. Atkinson, D.C.L. London (Macmillan), 1892.

delicately moulded and decorated vase of the type usually known as "incense cups" with its own proper deposit of incinerated remains and accompanying flints'. He then quotes the detailed description of it that he published in the *Gentleman's Magazine*: 'One inch in height and under one inch and a half in greatest diameter, of red ware, and scored with lines crossing one another diagonally, but so as to leave a space of three-eights of an inch all round, nearest to the bottom, untouched. It was placed mouth upwards, in the centre between four flints laid east, north, south, west, and comprising a very flat leaf-shaped arrow-point, another of the same description, but thicker, a thumb-flint or scraper, and some other implement; but all of them coarsely or rudely fashioned and chipped,—that is, as compared with many others found by the writer.'

The careful construction of the howes and the burial vessels associated with them are the only evidences of a civilization that prevailed for some centuries before it was destroyed by the invading Danes and Norwegians with their invincible bronze weapons. There seems to have been no mingling of the races such as took place between the Danes and the Normans (themselves a mixed race). The only trace of the 'Ancient British' are these desecrated howes, and that word was given to their graves by their conquerors (Danish: *hoj*).

Canon Atkinson, like his contemporary on the Wolds, Canon Greenwell, has had some hard words said about him for his un-systematic rifling of the howes, but I cannot leave him in bad odour. *Forty Years in a Moorland Parish* is a delightful book, and the personality of the man who walked more than 70,000 miles 'in the prosecution of his clerical work only' is very endearing. And his book lives as literature, and there are many pages in it that come near to the stylistic vividness of Hudson or Aksakoff. I will quote one of them:

'I was coming through the upper part of our Crag Wood one evening several years ago, after a day's shooting in Fryup, when, seeing a wild pigeon flying over my head and rather high up I fired, in the belief that it was within range. It fell to the shot, evidently killed on the instant. Falling from a considerable height, which was added to by the fact that it fell some little way below me on the very steep hill-side I was standing on, it dropped with great velocity, and the force with which it struck the ground—for the wood-pigeon is a weighty bird—was very considerable. I have written "struck the ground"; but in reality it struck a bare rock-fragment, and to my surprise I saw a sort of spring jet of brilliant scarlet objects sparkling upwards from the place of its fall. It lasted but a moment, of course; but it was striking enough for that moment. On going to pick the bird up, I found more than half a pint of holly-berries strewed all round it. The fact was, it had been getting its evening meal from among the many and large holly-trees which abound in the wood in question, and having filled its crop to repletion—you may see these birds' crops actually protrude from fulness as they fly past or over you on their way to their night's roosting-place—naturally it burst when the bird fell with such force against the hard rock.'

3

The Scarlet Chamber

Shortly after coming to Stonegrave the Rector handed me for safe keeping a small manuscript volume bound in leather. The binding, I afterwards ascertained, was probably Cambridge work of the seventeenth century, and it was, in fact, the commonplace book of a seventeenth-century Rector, Thomas Comber.* It had been presented to the church in 1936 by his great, great, great, great grandson, a clergyman in Cheshire. It is filled with minute but graceful writing easily legible, and the first forty-two and the last sixty pages are extracts in Latin, Greek, Hebrew and English from various theological writers. The intermediate pages are autobiographical: *The History of my Life: Collected Anno Domini: 1695 & 96*, followed, in Latin, by a *Brevis Narratio Vitae Meae*, and a *Theatrum Divinae Benevolentiae*.

The opening words of the English *Life* immediately engaged my sympathies: 'Being fixt by Providence in a remote country, 200 miles and above from the place of my nativity; I see fitt to give some account of myself, as well that I may not seem ungratefull for God's mercys: as that others may not be ignorant of my obligations to his providence.'

Thomas Comber was born at Westerham in Kent at the end of the year 1644 and he records the significant detail that he was the last child that was christened in the font at Westerham Church by the Common Prayer form 'which the Rebels then put down'. The Rebels were the Presbyterians under Cromwell, who defeated the King that same year at Naseby. The Comber family remained

---

* The commonplace book of Comber has been printed with other documents and memorials in the Publications of the Surtees Society, Vol. 156–7. Durham (Andrews & Co.), 1946–47. *The Autobiography of Mrs. Alice Thornton* is Vol. LXII (1875) in the same publications.

loyal to the King, and 'the rebellion growing hot', Comber's father was forced to fly into Flanders for four years, leaving the sickly infant in the care of a 'most dear, and indulgent mother'. Indeed, the infant Thomas was so weak that he was four years old before he could walk. But as soon as he could walk he went to an English school. Two years later he removed to a Latin master, a reverend and learned old gentleman named Mr. Thomas Walter, who had then a flourishing school at Westerham. This master 'grounded' Thomas in the Latin tongue, 'and having composed a Greek grammar, but being disabled by the palsy to transcribe it himself fair, he taught me to write, and read Greek, before I was ten years old'.

There followed brief intervals at a school in London, and at the great free school at Sevenoaks. After the inevitable disturbances of measles and smallpox, the boy, still only thirteen years old, was judged fit for the university, but on account of his being so very young, he remained with the minister at Westerham for another year, reading in 'choice Greek and Latin authors'. But then, at the age of fourteen, he was admitted to Sidney Sussex College, Cambridge, where he had a Reverend Edmund Mathews for his tutor, 'who lent him all sorts of books', and taught him privately 'all kinds of sciences and ingenious Arts; viz. experimentall Philosophy, Geometry & Astronomy, Painting, Musick, Dialling, and other parts of Mathematicks; and besides made me understand all the Orientall Tongues, and put me into an excellent method to reduce all that I should read in Philology and Divinity into Common places, of which I have found incredible benefit in all my studys'.

Comber made such good progress with his studies that after three years he took his Bachelor of Arts degree 'after a strict and public Examination . . . being not then eighteen years old'. He then spent some months studying at home, serving as a deacon to his old master the rector of Westerham (who had meanwhile removed to Staining), reading in Sion College library, until, in September of 1663, he was invited (by way of a friend of the Rector's) to come to Stonegrave as a curate.

He set out for Yorkshire on September 28, broke his journey at Cambridge (where he discovered, to his chagrin, that he had been passed over for a fellowship) and at Southwell (where Gilbert Bennet, the Rector of Stonegrave, was then incumbent), and finally reached Stonegrave on October 17. He was still only nineteen years old and had preached but twice before; but he mounted the pulpit with confidence and 'finding that I needed not write notes any more than the heads: I ventured to trust my memory for the matter, & my invention for the expressions, which as it gave great content to the people, so it gave me a great deal of time to study, which I did so employ, that I filled my Common Place Book in a few years time'.

The young curate who came to Stonegrave must have been singularly attractive in appearance and manners. A portrait of him is now in the church, given to the parish quite recently by a descendant of the family. It is probably the one which he describes as 'finished this day but will not be dry for a fortnight or so' in a letter he wrote from London on June 29, 1678—that is to say, in his thirty-fifth year. It depicts him with blue eyes and a fresh rosy complexion, the hair being long and wavy. The expression is candid, the brow smooth, and one would say that it represented a metaphysical poet rather than a divine.

The letter I have just mentioned was written to Madam Alice Thornton, the châtelaine of what was then the largest manor in the parish of Stonegrave, and whom by that time he could address as 'my dearest Mother'. When he arrived at Stonegrave the rectory was presumably still occupied by Mr. Bennet's family, so Comber found lodgings, at first in the village and later in the neighbouring hamlet of Ness (at that time within the parish). But Ness was two miles from the church and whether for this reason, or because the Thorntons were already prepossessed by his personal charm, they invited him, in March 1665, to take up his residence at East Newton (at not much less distance from the church). And there the young Comber found, not only 'for many years great opportunity of improving both in piety and all sorts of learning; it being a fine retirement, and yet affording me very choice company', but also, in the daughter of William and Alice Thornton, a wife.

Of this family we have an intimate account in the Autobiography of Alice Thornton which was for the first and only time published by the Surtees Society in 1875. It is a fascinating document which deserves to be better known, both as a family history of that time, and as a pious confession that reveals far more than it relates. Alice had been born at Kirklington on February 13,

1626-7, the daughter of Christopher Wandesford, a cousin of the Earl of Stafford, whom he accompanied on his mission to Ireland, and there became Lord Deputy. But he died in December, 1640, at the early age of 48. His widow maintained for a time the great household he had in Dublin, but in October of the next year 'that horrid rebellion and massacre of the poor English protestants began to break out in the country'. It is said that above forty thousand Protestants were butchered with almost every conceivable circumstance of cruelty; and in the immediate alarm Mrs. Wandesford took refuge with her children in Dublin castle. 'From thence we were forced into the cittie, continuing for fourteen days and nights in great fears, frights, and hideous distractions and disturbances from the alarms and outcries given in Dublin each night by the rebells, and with these frights, fastings, and pains about packing the goods and wanting sleep, times of eating, or refreshment, wrought so much upon my young body, that I fell into a desperate flux, called the Irish desease, being nigh unto death, while I stayed in Dublin, as also in the ship coming for England.' But thanks to the care and determination of her mother, Alice's young body survived all these endurances and the whole family disembarked at a beerhouse near Neston, in Cheshire, and stayed there several weeks.

As soon as Alice was well enough, the family moved from this beerhouse to Chester, and there they were beleaguered by the parliamentarians. But the siege was raised by a strange accident. Three 'grenadoes' were shot into the city. The first landed into the 'sconce' of the defenders, whereupon two men, 'having an oxe's hide ready, clapt it thereon, and it smothering away in shells did not spread, but went out'. The second landed short of the city, 'in a ditch within a pasture amongst a company of women milking, but was quenched without doing them harm. . . .' The last fell amongst their own horse, again short of the town, slaying many of them, and by that means the siege was raised. During the siege there had occurred one of those miraculous interventions of Providence for which Alice in her autobiography is always offering up devout thanks, 'Standing in a tirritt in my mother's house, having been at prayer in the first morning, we were beset in the town; and not hearing of it before, as I looked out at a window towards St. Mary's church, a cannon bullet flew so nigh the place where I stood that the window suddenly shut with such a force the whole tirritt shook; and it pleased God I escaped without more harm, save that the waft took my breath from me for that present, and caused a great fear and trembling, not knowing from whence it came.'

After several more 'passages and deliverances', for which the Lord is duly thanked, Mrs. Wandesford and her children set off with two trunks of wearing linen towards Yorkshire, passing through Warrington and Wigan (which they found 'sorely demolished, all the windows broken') and after some rough handling at the border, arrived at Snape, near Bedale, where Alice's sister Catherine, married to Sir Thomas Danby, was sheltering from the troubles. Mrs. Wandesford had the intention of living in York, where the two boys might be well educated; but the clash of arms had just reached that city and they were warned not to proceed. They found lodgings at Kirklington, not far from Hipswell, the dowager house of the family, which they went to as soon as it could be put in good repair. There they were troubled with the Scots one while, and the parliament forces another while, and for eighteen to twenty months were compelled to quarter the troops and endure their 'domineering & insulting voluptuousness'. Alice, who was now seventeen, was importuned by a Scots captain named Innes quartered on them, 'soe vild a bloody looked man, that I trembled all the time he was in the house', who plotted to kidnap her; and about the same time she had 'a great deliverance from the violence of a rape' from Jerimy Smithson, the son of a local baronet. She narrowly escaped drowning as she was crossing the Swale on horseback, a fate which befell her brother George in the same river seven years later.

King Charles I was beheaded on January 30, 1649, an event which Alice bemoans in eloquent and melancholy prose. The country began to settle down under Cromwell's stern rule, and Mrs. Wandesford, 'a desolate widow in times of desertion and troubles', now wished to see her daughter married. Her only remaining son Christopher was married to Sir John Lowther's daughter in September, 1651, and in the same year William Thornton presented himself as a suitor. Alice had no desire to give up her 'happy and free condition', but she was an obedient child and after much discussion of revenues and religion (Thornton's past being tainted with Presbyterianism), she submitted and was married on December 15 of that same year. But at two o'clock on that very day she 'fell suddenly so ill and sick after two o'clock in the afternoon, that I thought, and all that saw me did believe, it would have been my last night, being surprised with a violent pain in my head and stomach, causing a great vomiting and sickness at my heart, which lasted eight hours before I had any intermition'. Her mother attributed the fit to the fact that in preparation for the wedding she had been so incautious as to wash her feet at that time of the year.

The business of what Alice herself calls 'breeding' began at once and she was delivered of her first child on August 27 of the next year. The child, alas, did not live. A second child, a daughter named Alice, was born on January 3, 1654, and survived. A third born on February 14, 1655, died eighteen months later. A fourth child followed in June 1656, and a fifth, the first son, in December 1657. A second son was born in April, 1660, but died being scarce fourteen days old.

All these children were born at Hipswell, but meanwhile Thornton was rebuilding the family mansion at East Newton, which took six years and cost above £1,500, a large sum in those days. They moved in mid-June, 1662, and Alice describes how 'being great with child', she 'walked from Oswaldkirk with our company, having a great deal of strength and health given me from God'. The seventh child was born in September, and an eighth three years later, on September 23, 1665. By then the new curate was there to officiate at the thanksgiving; he had been in the house since March of that year, 'improving himself in his studies in this retired course of life'. Her husband, she says, 'took great delight in his facetious company and exercise of his religion, and ingenuity, and severall times would say to me and others that Mr. Comber, being a man that took such delight in his studies and learning so young, he was confident, being a man of such learning and parts, would come to great preferment in the church, if not to be a bishop'.

The new house must have been very beautiful. Two wings still survive, one serving as an unusually large farmhouse, the other as a barn. The middle range of the house has gone, and there are only some stone mullions to the windows of the fragmentary wings, and some panelled rooms within, to remind one of a former stateliness. But at the entrance to what is now the drive-in to the house there still stands a small square tower which was Comber's hermitage, and here he wrote the *Companion to the Temple* and other works of piety. From this tower he could look eastward up the dale, and it is only a few hundred yards across the meadows to the Rye, which here flows through deep banks with the sinuous and silvery vitality of a snake. The blue moors are in the distance, and here I love to wander with the ghost of Comber.

But if the Thorntons and the ingenious Comber found in this idyllic spot a refuge from civil wars and rebellions, their peace was soon to be disturbed by internal malice. Many pages of the *Autobiography* are taken up with an account of the affair, at once fulsome and confused. But the following is a reasonable reconstruction of the episode. Alice's elder sister Catherine, as already related, had married Sir Thomas Danby of Thorp Perrow and Masham. He had a second son Christopher, who in Virginia, without his father's consent, had married Anne Colepepper, niece of John, Lord Colepepper, Master of the Rolls. Anne was therefore Mrs. Thornton's niece by marriage, and being left a widow at some time before this, and being out of favour with her father-in-law, had received much kindness from her aunt. We first hear of her as godmother to Mrs. Thornton's ninth child, baptized at Newton on November 11, 1667 (the child died three weeks later). She was presumably staying at Newton at this time, and then met Thomas Comber. At any rate, as Alice Thornton admits, two years later Anne was then 'his great friend (pretended so, however), whose advice he was ever inclined to observe, as from a wise and prudent friend'. But the advice she tended Comber did not suit Alice Thornton. For whatever reason, Mrs. Danby was determined to detach Comber from the Thorntons, and marry him to a woman of her own choice, a Mrs. Mary Batt whom she brought to Newton with that intention. Madame Thornton had countered with a proposal that Comber should marry her own daughter Alice, who at that time was only fourteen years old. Events reached a climax one day in a panelled room called the Scarlet Chamber at Newton, where Mrs. Danby and her servant were staying. Mrs. Danby accused her aunt of wishing to marry Comber to her child to cover her own illicit relations with him. 'By these lyes I was ruined and brought to a public scorn, as poor Susanna was before the judges who was wronged by the false witness of two wicked Elders. Even so was I and my poor child accused and condemned before her in her chamber by her servant in a most notorious manner, and all my chaste life and conversation most wickedly traduced, so that she railed on me and scolded at me and my poor innocent child, before our faces, with the most vile expressions could be imagined . . . I was so extremely tormented with these slanders that I mourned and wept so extremely, with her loud clamours against us, that my dear husband, being then walking in the hall, heard the sad tragedy and abuse was put on me, and in a great anger he came to the door of the scarlet chamber and broke it open, and hearing my complaint, and seeing my condition, did kick that wench down stairs, and turn her out in a great rage for so wickedly doing against us; and had certainly kicked out Mrs. Danby too, but that I begged he would not, because she had no house or harbour to go to, and I trusted God would revenge my cause.'

The exact date of this scene is not given, but it was probably in the summer of 1668. Both Alice Thornton and her husband were physically upset by the calumnies. Alice says that by September she 'had fallen into a very great and dangerous condition of sickness, weakness of body, and afflicted mind, with excess of grief thereon'. But the condition of her husband must have been worse for he died suddenly of a palsy while on a visit to Malton, on September 17. Exactly two months later, on November 17, Comber was secretly married to the daughter Alice in 'that very chamber in which Mrs. Danby had been hatching and contriving all her malice against us three'. 'This business was transacted with great gravity and piety, after which my daughter and myself went to prayer, to beg a blessing and a mercy upon our great undertaking . . . the bridegroom, as in those cases, laid down a wedding-ring and several pieces of gold, as a token of his faithful and conjugal love to his dear bride, over whom he expressed abundance of joy and inward satisfaction to have obtained so virtuous and chaste a wife of God. . . .'

Why was such a great undertaking kept secret for a time? Mrs. Thornton tells us that an 'abominable beast, Mr. Tankred, who envied anyone's chastity . . . had laid a wager with my dear Lady Yorke of £100, that if my husband were dead I would be married within a month to Mr. Comber'. Tankred's malice, she explains, was due to her having disappointed him on the foreclosure of a

mortgage he held on Leysthorpe, land adjoining East Newton—
she had cleared the mortgage in time. All the more reason, one
might conclude, that Tankred should be openly thwarted in
the matter of the wager. 'By reason of our adversaries' malice,'
is the illogical reason for secrecy given by Mrs. Thornton; but
she also explains that the publication of the event would have been
'too near the time of my sorrow and great mourning for my dear
husband, it was by consent thought fit that the solemnity of the
getting the bride to bed should be deferred till it was convenient
to invite all Mr. Thornton's relations to the publication of their
marriage'. This event took place six months later, on May 19,
1669, when many friends and neighbours were invited to 'as
handsome an entertainment as I could be able to procure, con-
sidering my own weakness and ill habit of health'. 'At night they
had also a good supper, and those usual solemnities of marriage,
of getting the bride to bed, with a great deal of decency and
modesty of all parties was this solemnity performed.' Comber
himself was moved to write the following poem:

> Have you not seen the glorious sun,
> After the darksome night was gone,
> Nimbly climb up the azure sky,
> Scattring his beams of majesty;
> Rejoicing mortals every where,
> Who long had wish'd he would appear?
> O! What a smile doth seem to sit
> On ev'ry brow to welcome it;
> And glowing Phaebus whips amain
> His weary steeds to mount the plain;
> Disbanding all the mists of night,
> Filling the world with joy and light.
> Just such a welcome waits upon
> Th'appearance of my lovely one.
> Make haste, dear love, oh! do not stay,
> Nor in adorning spend this day!
> Your beauteous form was dress'd before
> With virtue, piety, and store
> Of all attractive charming graces;
> And these are more to me than laces,
> Pendents or jewels, knots or rings;

THE SCARLET CHAMBER

Let those who from these trifling things
Do borrow all their worth, take care
Of these: thou need'st them not my fair!

Comber's bride was born on January 5, [n.s. 1654]. She was therefore still only fourteen years old at the time of her marriage, and there may have been some scruple against publishing the marriage of a child of this age. Comber himself, in the *History* of his life, says that 'to prevent my moving back to the South, Madame Thornton had given consent that I should have her daughter Mrs. Alice; and as I had been a means to secure her fortune and her sister's during her Father's life: so she finding me likely to be more serviceable to the family after his death (the heir being but 7 years old, and the daughters being both very young) resolved to grant my request, and gave me leave by licence from York, *privately* to marry my now dear wife, her eldest daughter Mrs. Alice: the marriage being made at Newton, November 17 in this year by Mr. Charles Man, but was not made public *for some reasons* till May 17th in the next year'. The reasons remain unstated: I can only conclude that Madame Thornton was determined to retain Comber, that Comber was not unwilling to be retained, and that the means Madame Thornton used were such that they could not be immediately made public without aggravating the scandal that prevailed.

The marriage was a happy one. It was not until five years later that a first son was born and then 'the infant expired as soon as it was born and could not be baptized'. Meanwhile Comber in his turret had completed his first book, *A Companion to the Temple*, and his mother had visited him in Newton, 'had read and heard many divers sheets before her death to her abundant comfort'. She died at Newton and was buried on the right hand of the altar at Stonegrave; a brass plate that Comber had made to record her virtues is still in place.

William Thornton seems to have been thriftless and incompetent in affairs. Alice was left with a large house and little money, and most of the remaining pages of her autobiography are taken up with an account of her afflictions. Her brother, Sir Charles Wandesford, turned against her and compelled her to strip herself of all the arrears due to her; there is much talk of rent-charges and mortgages, of great taxes, sessments and public charges, and of what should be sold to pay her husband's debts. Even the great bed in the scarlet chamber, 'being a very rich flowered silk damask bed, with all answerable to it of the same, and a large one . . . a noble down bed, with bolsters, pillows, blankets and all suitable', even this prized possession was impounded.

But Madame Thornton bore it all with Christian fortitude and with many prayers to God's almighty power to bring her out of it all. 'My poor ability,' she says, 'was in teaching my dear and only son to read, and hear him his catechism, prayers and psalms, getting proverbs by heart, and many such like duties. But one day, above all the rest, being as I remember, on my own birthday, in the afternoon, having kept the other part separate in fasting and prayer, February 13, 1668–9—as I was sitting on the long settle in my chamber, and hearing read in the gospel of St. Matthew, my heart was full of sorrow and bitterness of spirit, being overwhelmed with all sorts of afflictions that lay upon me, considering my poor condition, either to pay debts, to maintain this poor young child, or to give him the education which I would, and designed, by God's blessing, to bring him up a clergyman, and a true minister of the gospel . . . Such was my sad condition at this time, that passion and a flood of tears overcame my reason and my religion, and made me to leave my dear child when I was teaching him to read, and could not contain my great and infinite sorrows, but scarce got to my bedside for falling down, when I then cast myself across the bed, fell in bitter weeping and extreme passion for offending God, or provoking his wrath against me, to leave and forsake me thus forlorn. But while I was in this desperate condition, and full of despair in myself, behold the miraculous goodness of God, even the God who I apprehended had forsaken me and cast me off for ever, in that very instant of time did bring me an unexpected both relief and comfort, tho' a mixture of His gentle reproof for my too great passion and impatience under His hand and correction. My dear son Robert, seeing me fallen down on the bed in such a sad condition and bitter weeping, comes to me to the bedside, and being deeply concerned to see me in such extremity, crept on the bed with his poor hands and knees, and cast himself on my breast, and imbracing me in his arms, and laid his cheek to mine with abundance of tears, cried out to me in these words: "Oh! my dear, sweet mother; what is the reason that you do weep and lament and mourn so much, and ready to break your heart? Is it for my father that you do mourn so much?" To which I answered: "Oh! my dear child, it is for the loss of thy dear father. Have I not cause? for I am this day a desolate widow left, and thou art a poor young orphant without help or any relief." To which my dear infant answered, "Do you not, my dear mother, believe that my father is gone to heaven?" To which I replied again, "Yes, I do believe and hope through Christ's merits and sufferings for us that thy dear father is gone to heaven." Upon which he said to me again, "And would you have my father to come out of heaven, where he enjoys God, and all joy and happiness, to come down out of heaven and indure all those sickness and sorrows he did, to comfort you here? Who is the father of the fatherless, and husband to the widow? Is not God? Will He not provide for you? Oh! my dear mother, do not weep and lament thus very sore, for if I live I will take care for you and comfort you, but if you weep thus, and mourn, you will break my heart, and then all is gone; therefore, my dear mother, be comforted in God, and He will preserve you." All which words, uttered with so great a compassion, affection, and filial dearness and tenderness, can never be forgot by me. But this excellent counsel came from God, and not from man; for none but the Spirit of God could put such words into the mouth of a child but six years old and four months.'

There is one other incident which completes the self portrait of this good woman, which must again be told in her own words. About March 25, 1669, she had begun to recover her strength and was writing the First Book of her Life, as she calls it. 'There was a poor little creature, harmless in itself, and without any gall or malice to do hurt, a little young chicken not above fourteen days old, which had been exposed, and picked out of the hen's nest that hatched it, and by her was turned out from amongst the flock she had newly hatched, being about nine in number. All which she brooked, and made much of, but this poor chick she had turned out of the nest in a morning when the maid came to see if she was hatched; and finding this poor chicken cast out of the nest on the ground and for dead and cold; but the maid took it up and put it under the hen, to have recruited it by warmth. But the hen was so wild and mad at it, that she would not let it be with her or come near her, but picked it, and bit it, and scratched it out with her feet twice or thrice when the maid put it in, so that she saw no hopes of the hen to nurse it up as the rest, so she took it up and put it in her breast to recover it. And so she brought this poor creature to me, and told me all this story with great indignation against the unnaturalness of its mother. But I, pitying this forlorn creature in that case, could not withhold my care, to see if I could any way save the life of it, and carried it to the fire, wrapped it in wool, and got some cordial waters and opened its bill and put a drop by little and little, and then it gasped and came to life within an hour, giving it warm milk, till it was recovered and became a fine pert chicken.

'Thus I saved it and recovered it again, making much of it, and was very fond of it, having recovered it to life, and kept it in a basket with wool in the nights, and in my pocket in the days, till it came to be a very pretty coloured and a strong bird, about fourteen or sixteen days old, and sometimes put it into my bosom to nourish and bring it up, hoping it had been a hen chick, and then I fancied it might have brought me eggs in time, and so get a breed of it. This was my innocent diversion in my melancholy hours; till one day, about Candlemas, 1669, having begun a book wherein I had entered very many and great remarks of my course of life . . . I took out this poor chicken out of my pocket to feed it with bread, and set it on the table besides me. It picking about the bread, innocently did peep up at my left eye. Whether it thought the white of my eye had been some bread, while I was intent on my book, in writing held my head and eye down, not suspecting any hurt, or fearing any evil accident, this poor little bird picked one pick at the white of my left eye, as I looked downward, which did so extremely smart and ache that I could not look up, or see of either of my eyes. And the pain and the blood-shot of it grew up into a little knot or lump, with the hurt and bruise in that tender part, that I was sore swelled and blood-shot, that it took away the sight of it for a long time, and had a skin and pearl of it, and with pain and sickness brought me to my bed, and I could not see almost anything of it, and endangered the sight of both . . .'

Instead of bemoaning her lot, Madame Alice thanks God for his great mercy in preserving her right eye, and after six weeks or more of suffering, in restoring the sight of her left eye. And then comes the end of the story, which is so revealing of this woman's goodness of heart. 'Nor could I suffer this poor creature to be killed, as I was put upon for this, for it did it in its innocency. There was some who jested with me, and said, they had heard of an old saying of "bringing up a chicken to pick out their eye". But now they saw I had made good that old saying, both in this bird, and what harm I had suffered from Mrs. Danby, of whom I had been so careful, and preserved her and hers from starving. But I told you that her crime was more impardonable, for what was done by her was out of malice, and unmerited from me; and what I did for hers and her was out of my Christian charity, and God's cause; and only of pity I saved that dying chicken.'

Madame Thornton's autobiography ends with this year 1669, and almost with this incident; but she lived on, always at East Newton. Comber settled down to an assiduous career in the Church. He had many preferments, became first a prebend and then precentor at York, Chaplain-in-ordinary to Queen Anne and afterwards to William and Mary, and finally (1691) Dean of Durham. He wrote many polemical works against the Papists and the Quakers, *A Discourse on Duels* and *A Historical Vindication of the Divine Right of Tithes*. A bibliography of his published writings amounts to forty-two items. But throughout this career he remained Rector of Stonegrave, and a faithful friend and pro-tector of Madame Thornton. He died at East Newton on Nov-ember 25, 1699, at the early age of fifty-five, and against a for-feiture was 'buried in linen' (instead of wool, as prescribed by an Act of 1666 intended for the encouragement of the woollen trade) in the choir of Stonegrave Church, where a large black marble slab still marks his resting-place, and is engraved with a long and eloquent tribute to this *Vir Pietate, Eruditione, Ingenio, Judicio, Caeterisque Animi Dotibus Clarus*. 'I am come to lay my bones near you and my other mother,' he announced to Madame Thornton.

Madame Thornton survived, not only Comber, but Robert, her only surviving son, who had died in 1692; and even her grandson, Comber's son William, who died in 1703. As the years passed she seems to have been stripped of everything but her noble and now empty house. Her will, which she made in 1705, contains a long list of her gifts to Stonegrave church, mostly perishable textiles. Her 'harpsicall virginalls' she left to her dear daughter Comber for her life with her wedding ring and a gold seal. She left the sum of twenty pounds for the rebuilding of the chapel at East

Newton, 'which was long since demolished', and 'unto the chapel to be rebuilded, my great brass pot of bell metal to be cast into a bell, and there to remain for ever'.

But the chapel was never to be rebuilt nor the metal cast into a bell. Alice Thornton's own grave in Stonegrave Church is a plain slab of stone with no record of her many virtues and charities, but her name only and the date: ALICE THORNTON 1706. Comber's son Thomas continued to live at East Newton until he died in 1765; and his son, also Thomas, born in 1722, who was a Doctor of Laws of Jesus College, Cambridge, and Rector of Buckworth and Morbourne, was buried at Stonegrave in 1778. It was this grandson of Comber's who found among the medieval manuscripts that had lain in East Newton since the dissolution of the Cistercian Monastery of Rievaulx, a volume which aroused his curiosity and which he eventually sold (perhaps with the estate?) to the Earl of Feversham at Duncombe Park. This was the *Centum Sententiae* of Walter Daniel, monk of Rievaulx, which contains the life of his master, the Abbot Ailred, a document of great interest and charm with which I shall be concerned in the next chapter.

East Newton must have been abandoned as a gentleman's residence about this time and allowed to fall into ruin; from which ruins the present farmhouse was redeemed; and by some chance, though in bad state, Comber's turret.

4

Saint Ailred

A little more than ten miles from each end, Stonegrave lies half-way on a straight line drawn from Rievaulx Abbey to the palace built by Sir John Vanbrugh for the Earl of Carlisle at Castle Howard. Castle Howard has no place in my childhood memories, and I cannot remember when I first visited it. But these two edifices gradually began to assume a symbolic significance for me, perhaps sharpened some years later by a reading of Henry Adams's *Mont-St.-Michel and Chartres*. This book was published in 1913, and I must have read it during, or shortly after, the First World War. It was the first intimation I had of the mediatory function of architecture. When Adams wrote of Chartres that it expressed an emotion—'the deepest man ever felt—the struggle of his own littleness to grasp the infinite', I knew at once, from my early experiences at Rievaulx, what he meant. I now think that Adams was addicted to the pathetic fallacy. He combined to a dangerous degree two qualities that usually destroy each other—sentiment and intellect (to be clearly distinguished from sensibility and intelligence). *Mont-St.-Michel and Chartres* is a Sentimental Journey by a man with a scientific mind (and one might say the same of his masterpiece, *The Education of Henry Adams*). This queasy American had come to the conclusion that 'the twelfth and thirteenth centuries, studied in the pure light of political economy, are insane', and the reason he found, oddly enough, in their effeminacy. It was an epoch dominated by Queens, and above all by the Queen of Heaven, the Virgin. 'The scientific mind is atrophied' in such a female world— 'suffers under inherited cerebral weakness, when it comes in contact with the enternal woman Astarte, Isis, Demeter, Aphrodite, and the last and greatest deity of all, the Virgin . . . the study of Our Lady, as shown by the art of Chartres, leads directly back to Eve, and lays bare the whole subject of sex.'

It certainly laid bare, however unwittingly, the whole subject of Henry Adams, but I shall not pursue it here. Perhaps Adams did little more than elaborate certain of Ruskin's insights about the place of woman in the development of civilization and about the conflict of technology and humanism. Adams found his symbol for technology in the dynamo, and he thought that the cathedrals had been in some ways more industrial than religious. 'The mere masonry and structure made a vast market for labour; the fixed metal-work and woodwork were another; but the decoration was by far the greatest. The wood-carving, the glass-windows, the sculpture, inside and out, were done mostly in workshops on the spot, but besides these fixed objects, precious works of the highest perfection filled the church treasuries.' And all this manufacture was in aid of the Virgin, a vast world's fair of votive offerings.

Adams made a precise distinction between expression and construction, and in Chartres the construction had been subordinated to expression—to a celebration of the personal presence of the Virgin. If you would argue that Light, too, had symbolic value, as the visible emanation of Godhead, and that Suger, in interpreting St. Augustine and the Pseudo-Dionysus, was making the construction serve this more abstract conception, Adams would have maintained that the same light was nevertheless required to illuminate the Virgin as she travelled into darker latitudes. Paris or Laon might be ambiguous, but the church at Chartres belonged 'not to the people, not to the priesthood, and not even to Rome; it belonged to the Virgin . . . the Chartres apse shows the same genius that is shown in the Chartres rose; the same large mind that overrules—the same strong will that defies difficulties. The Chartres apse is as entertaining as all other Gothic apses together, because it overrides the architect. You may, if you really have no imagination whatever, reject the idea that the Virgin herself made the plan; the feebleness of our fancy is now congenital, organic, beyond stimulant or strychnine, and we shrink like sensitive-plants from the touch of a vision or spirit; but at least one can still sometimes feel a woman's taste, and in the apse of Chartres one feels nothing else'. But another and more recent commentator, Otto von Simson, finds in that same nave 'that virile, somewhat coarse-grained genius which characterizes the work of the master of Chartres throughout'. And adds: 'Obviously, both the master and his stone were natives of the same soil.'*

All this may only prove that symbols are multivalent, but I take it as a warning against giving any general validity to my own subjective associations with Rievaulx. That these are sentimental cannot be denied. The setting of the abbey is sufficient in itself to induce a mood of quiet devotion. When Dorothy Wordsworth and William visited it on the way to Brompton where the poet was married to Mary Hutchinson in 1802, 'thrushes were singing, cattle were feeding among green-grown hillocks about the ruins. These hillocks were scattered over with *grovelets* of wild roses and other shrubs, and covered with wild flowers. I could have stayed in this solemn quiet spot till evening, without a thought of moving, but William was waiting for me . . .' The abbey stands in what Dorothy called 'a larger valley among a brotherhood of valleys', and its precise geometry seems like some crystalline symbol of the natural beauty around it. I believe the beauty of the construction is demonstrably rhythmical or harmonical—mathematical, in fact. The abbey, like Chartres or any other church of the period, was no doubt 'designed and experienced as a representation of an ultimate reality', but it is the representation that is experienced, not the ultimate reality. All our symbols are intermediaries, bridges thrown across a great chasm, and they do not move the divided mountains. It is the structure of the bridge that becomes the reality, announcing a connection between the known and the unknown.

Though Daniel's *Sentences*, which I am about to mention, were at East Newton in Comber's time, probably with other manuscripts from the despoiled abbey, he does not anywhere mention Rievaulx. He probably associated if with the sect against which he directed so much of his polemical zeal, and thought of it as well out of the way. But if he had read the *Sentences*, and had been able to abate his prejudice, he would have found in the personality of Ailred, as lovingly depicted by Walter Daniel, a kindred spirit.

Daniel's *Vita Ailredi* was acquired by the Rylands Library in 1914, and only in 1950, the year after I came to Stonegrave, was it published in the original text with an English translation by

* *The Gothic Cathedral: Origins of Gothic Architecture and the Medieval Concept of Order.* By Otto von Simson. New York (Bollingen Series) and London (Routledge & Kegan Paul), 1956.

Professor Powicke.* I have never felt so grateful to a scholar or to a publisher, for this volume not only reconstitutes the abbey in all its early and pure enthusiasm, but also brings us into the living presence of a saint. How much I am indebted to Professor Powicke will be obvious in the following pages.

Ailred was a Northumbrian, a son of Eilaf of Hexham, a married priest with land and good connections. He was born in 1110, his father being a friend and ally of King David of Scotland. David's son Henry was his childhood companion. 'I lived with him from the cradle; we grew up together in boyhood; we knew each other in our adolescence,' Ailred was afterwards to relate. Walter Daniel tells us that the King was so fond of Ailred that he made him great in his house and glorious in his palace. He was made 'echonomus' or steward in the royal household and 'nothing, inside or out, was done without him'. He stood in the presence of the King at dinner, but often, when 'serving the dishes and dividing the food in turn to the eaters, his thoughts would be in the other world, and oblivious to outward things, as one caught up in an ecstasy to the heavenly heights, he would forget the affairs of the belly in a pleasant excess of contemplation on the apostolic words: "Meats for the belly, and belly for meats: but God shall destroy both it and them." For he practised from his boyhood spareness of living'. Daniel tells us much more of the modesty and decency of the young Ailred: such as, that he 'avoided elaborate confections, as the wear of the proud and effeminate; his dress consisted of an ordinary toga and a cloak, each as simply and sparely cut as was consistent with decency'.

In 1134 Ailred came to the neighbourhood of York, on an official visit to the archbishop. In the neighbourhood was Waldef, King David's stepson and a companion of his youth, who by this time had become prior of Kirkham Abbey. It was probably from this close friend that he learned how certain monks, some two years before, had come to England from across the sea and established a monastery in the valley of the Rye—'white monks by name and white also in vesture—for . . . as the angels might be,

* *The Life of Ailred of Rievaulx*, by Walter Daniel. Translated from the Latin. with Introduction and Notes by F. M. Powicke, F.B.A. London (Nelson) 1950.

I would like to pay my tribute, not only to the scholarship of Sir Maurice Powicke, for which he is justly esteemed, but also to the beauty of his prose style.

they were clothed in undyed wool spun and woven from the pure fleece of the sheep. So named and garbed and gathered together like flocks of sea-gulls,* they shine as they walk with the whiteness of snow'.

These monks from Citeaux in Normandy had come to Yorkshire at the invitation of Walter Espec, one of Henry the First's leading barons, a gigantic man who lived in the castle at Helmsley (which is the market town on the Rye between Stonegrave and Rievaulx). Espec had turned pious in his old age, and was eventually to end his days as a monk in the abbey he had founded. The monks 'set up their huts' on a site skilfully chosen for its beauty and convenience. Daniel is as eloquent as Dorothy Wordsworth about it: 'High hills surround the valley, encircling it like a crown. These are clothed by trees of various sorts and maintain in pleasant retreats the privacy of the vale, providing for the monks a kind of second paradise of wooded delights. From the loftiest rocks the waters wind and tumble down to the valley below, and as they make their hasty way through the lesser passages and narrower beds and spread themselves in wider rills, they give out a gentle murmur of soft sound and join together in the sweet notes of a delicious melody.'

According to Daniel, Ailred was so excited by the story of these monks that he rushed back to his lodging, mounted his horse and with the hastiest of farewells to his hosts, galloped off to Helmsley castle (twenty-four miles frcm York) which he reached before nightfall. Lord Walter welccmed him, told him more about the monks, and the next day he was taken to Rievaulx to visit them. Ailred was moved to tears by all he saw and heard, but returned that day to Helmsley castle and spent another night there. The next morning he set off with his servants on horseback to rejoin the court of the King in Scotland. But the road north from Helmsley leads past the place where a very steep path descends to Rievaulx, and there Ailred paused, and asked one of his servants whether he would like to go down to the abbey again and learn something more than he had seen the day before. The servant said, 'I am for going down,' so down they went and Ailred never came up again as a layman. 'He divided all his goods, he abandoned everything that he had. He kept beside him only the

* Flocks of sea-gulls are still a common sight in Ryedale—they fly in from the coast thirty miles to the east.

one man of his company who was willing to stay. As he owned to me afterwards, the four days of waiting where he was were like a thousand years, so great was his longing and haste to be taken to the novice's cell. He had no eyes for the light of day; all that time he saw only the horror of night.'

So began a warfare, as Daniel calls it, 'adorned with the three marks of the monastic life, holy contemplation, sincere prayer and honest toil'. Or, in more picturesque language, 'like a busy bee flitting about the meadows of virtue, he filled the store-room of his heart with three sorts of things, honey, oil and butter; the honey of the contemplation by which he drank in the pleasures of heaven, the oil of piety which made him shine, the butter of compassion for his neighbour, for whose sins he poured out his prayers to God'.

Ailred rose rapidly in the esteem of the abbot, William, so rapidly that nine years later, in 1143, he was sent to Rome to plead before the Pope the case of the Cistercians in the North of England, who had raised objections to the appointment of a new Archbishop of York, accusing the candidate and the responsible canons of simony (this archbishop was later to be canonized as Saint William of York). On his return, Ailred was made master of novices, and in this same year was sent into Lincolnshire to establish a monastery at Revesby. He returned to Rievaulx in 1147 and began to write that work which Walter Daniel considered the best of all his works, the *Speculum Caritatis*. It was at this time 'he had built a small chamber of brick under the novice-house, like a little tank, into which water flowed from hidden rills. Its opening was shut by a very broad stone in such a way that nobody would notice it. Ailred would enter this contrivance, when he was alone and undisturbed, and immerse his whole body in the icy cold water, and so quench the heat in himself of every vice'.

William, the first abbot of Rievaulx, who had been St. Bernard's secretary at Clairvaux, died in 1145. His place was taken by a monk called Maurice, but he retired two years later, and then Ailred was chosen for the office. He was now thirty-seven years old, but already afflicted by stone in the bladder, from which he was to suffer abominably for the remaining twenty years of his life. Of Ailred's many good works Daniel gives good account. Under his rule Rievaulx doubled in size and in activity—'indeed, he trebled the intensity of the monastic life and its charity. On feast days you might see the church crowded with the brethren like bees in a hive, unable to move forward because of the multitude, clustered together, rather, and compacted into one angelical body'. When he died in 1167 the community consisted of 140 monks and 500 *conversi* (lay brothers proper) and laymen (hired servants).

Daniel gives vivid descriptions of Ailred's sufferings in the last ten years of his life, by which time arthritis had been added to his old distress. 'So dreadfully afflicted was he that I have seen him suspended in mid-air in a linen sheet, held by a man at each of its four corners, being carried to relieve himself or from one bed to another. A mere touch affected him like a piercing wound, and his cries revealed the measure of his pains.' He had a cot constructed from which he could interview his brethren or dictate his letters and sermons. In that abode of his, says Daniel, he wrote many memorable works. He also performed miraculous cures, the titles of which are eloquent enough,—the monk with a stomachic disease who became dumb, the shepherd who was dumb for three days, the young monk with heart failure who lost the use of his faculties, the young man who swallowed a frog while drinking some water to quench his thirst ('and which had grown in his belly and eaten away his entrails day by day, gathering thence by what it lived')—all these he restored immediately to perfect health.

In his last years Ailred grew very emaciated—'hardly any flesh clung to his bones; his lips alone remained, a frame to his teeth'. He spent his time in prayer and vigils, and in reading the Confessions of Augustine, 'for it was these that had been his guide when he was converted from the world'. The light of angelic visitation would shine upon his head, and 'he talked with heavenly spirits just as he was wont to talk with men; and when he was alone there many voices used to be heard there, and that place became very dreadful'. A racking cough was next added to his afflictions, and he found difficulty in breathing. But he still occasionally preached to the brethren, and Daniel mentions in particular one sermon 'crowned with a proem of deep humility, delivered from the heart to the heart, and with much fatigue of body'. On his death bed he ordered to be brought to him his glossed psalter, the Confessions of Augustine, and the text of John's gospel, the relics of certain saints and a little cross that had belonged to Henry Murdac, Archbishop of York. He lived for ten days without food, but with senses unimpaired. The monks stood about him, now twelve, now twenty, now forty, now even a hundred—'so vehemently was this lover of us all loved by us'. Hasten, hasten, he cried to the angels that were waiting to receive his soul; 'and often he drove the word home by calling on the name of Christ in English, a word of one syllable in this tongue and easier to utter, and in some ways sweeter to hear'. And then Daniel interrupts his Latin text to give these words in English: 'Festinate, for crist luve.' *Luve* is how this word is still pronounced in Rievaulx.

'He died about the fourth watch of the night before the Ides of January, in the year of the Incarnation one thousand one hundred and sixty-six, which was the fifty-seventh year of his life. When his body was laid naked before us to be washed, we saw how the glory to come had been revealed in the father. His flesh was clearer than glass, whiter than snow, as though his members were those of a boy of five years old, without a trace of stain, but altogether sweet, and composed and pleasant. There was no loss of hair to make him bald, his long illness had caused no distortion, fasting no pallor, tears had not bleared his eyes. Perfect in every part of his body, the dead father shone like a carbuncle, was fragrant as incense, pure and immaculate in the radiance of his flesh as a child.'

Ailred's bones still lie under the grass in the ruined choir. No doubt many good and holy monks and abbots lived after his time in Rievaulx, but it is only Ailred's presence that is still palpable— Why? He was against the spirit of romance and I do not wish to idealize him in a romantic spirit. Professor Powicke allows himself one interesting speculation. A casual reference in the *Speculum Caritatis* suggests that Ailred was familiar with the Arthurian legend. A novice had confessed to him that he had often shed tears over the story of a certain Arthur. It is also recorded that Walter Espec in Helmsley once borrowed Geoffrey Monmouth's *Historia Regum* for Dame Cunstance, wife of Ralf fit Gilbert, Lord of Scampton, who was helping Gaimar to collect materials for his *Lestorie des Engles*. We know that wandering *conteurs* were about in the North Riding, for the counts of Brittany had long ruled in Richmond. Ailred could not foresee, suggests Professor Powicke, that 'the Arthurian legend would give the sanction of beauty to most of those earthly joys which he (Ailred) was training his novices to forget. The spirit of romance, a mightier influence than St. Bernard's, was abroad. In the course of time it has submitted even monks and cloisters to its fancies. Today it reigns in the place where Ailred taught, and waves its magic wand over the ruins of Rievaulx'.

It was the same magic wand that waved over the boy of 'The Innocent Eye'. But now I see in Ailred something more substantial, something he would not have disowned, something not at all to the Virgin's taste, as interpreted by Henry Adams. Two of Ailred's principal writings, the *Speculum Caritatis* (1142-3) and the *De Spirituali amicitia* (c. 1160) are largely concerned with friendship, and there can be no doubt that friendship was an emotional as well as a spiritual necessity for him. Throughout the *Speculum*, Professor Powicke tells us, 'he seems to have been sustained by the sweet and solemn sense of obligation to two close friendships: one—the greatest friendship of his life—for a monk called Simon, who had recently died, and to whom he devotes in his book a moving chapter; the other to the prior Hugh, who had left Rievaulx'. Simon, a 'model young man, well born, beautiful and holy, may possibly have been the Simon de Sigillo, whose psalter was preserved in the following century in the library. . . .' There was a later and younger friend, whose name is not known but who may have been Geoffrey of Dinant, who became Ailred's confidant and finally sub-prior, who also died before the dialogue on friendship was written.

Spiritual friendship is not to be confused with physical attraction, but as Plato first so beautifully demonstrated, such friendship is a great daemon that holds an intermediate place between what is divine and what is mortal, and that is how Ailred experienced it. His ideal was masculine, brotherly, communal, and that is why I find it difficult to think of the Virgin as the dictator of his taste.

It is true that Rievaulx was dedicated to St. Mary the Virgin, and this presumably from the time of its foundation. But Ailred was a Northumbrian, and his favourite saint was St. Cuthbert— while he journeyed to the general chapter at Citeaux or visited the daughter-houses of Rievaulx in Scotland, Ailred, Professor Powicke tells us, put himself under the protection of St. Cuthbert. St. Cuthbert's Cathedral at Durham is the most masculine building in Christendom.

A DEARTH OF WILD FLOWERS

Among the many tributes to love in the *Speculum Caritatis* is one which clearly illustrates its meaning for Ailred: 'The other day when I was going round the cloister garth of the monastery, the brethren were seated together like a crown that is most dear to me; it was as though I were amid the liveliness of Paradise and I kept admiring the flowers and leaves and fruits of each of the trees, and I found no one in that multitude whom I did not love and by whom I was not confident that I was loved. I was suffused with a joy so great that it surpassed all the delights of the world. For I felt my spirit transfused into all and that the affection of all had passed over into me, so that I said with the prophet: "Behold how good and how pleasant it is for brethren to dwell together in unity." '*

The building of the church at Rievaulx was begun in 1145, twelve years before Ailred died. The original transepts remain nearly to their full height on the west, and have plain round-headed windows in a style still Romanesque, but the eastern arm of the church was built in the new and more graceful style during the second quarter of the thirteenth century, fifty years after Ailred's death. Chartres, which must have been familiar to the architect of Rievaulx, was built between 1194 and 1220 under strong Platonist influence—a Neoplatonic tradition had been established there as early as the eleventh century by Bishop Fulbert. John of Salisbury, 'the most famous of all the bishops of Chartres', was not only a Platonist who believed in the ethical value of music, but he was also in sympathy with the Cistercian movement. At Chartres the laws of musical harmony were deliberately applied to architecture. At Rievaulx too.

At the Suppression there were three chapels in the presbytery, dedicated to Our Lady, St. John the Baptist and St. John the Evangelist, each containing a gilded image. But that was nearly four centuries later: there were no such chapels in Ailred's time, and certainly no gilded images. In *Speculum Caritatis* Ailred denounces all such extravagances. But long before the Suppression Ailred's spirit was dead, the spirit of Plato was dead, the spirit of Saint Augustine was dead. The stones might still vibrate with silent music but there were no ears to hear them, and they might therefore be left to perish. But for those whose minds have been

---

* Trans. by T. Edmund Harvey, *Saint Aelred of Rievaulx*. London, 1932, pp. 91–2.

attuned to the divine philosophy, even in this late day there are a few melancholy notes to be heard in the bare ruined choir—in the early morning, before the coaches arrive, or in the twilight, long after they have departed.

5

Alas, Poor Yorick!

Four miles to the south of Rievaulx, divided by steep wooded scars and a high bare moor, are the ruins of a second Cistercian abbey, Byland. Less complete than Rievaulx, and not so cunningly sited, these ruins are nevertheless all that is left of a monastery that was once the equal of Rievaulx, and, indeed, one of the most elaborate ecclesiastical buildings in England. The abbey church had the same length as Beverley Minster and it may have been the largest of all the Cistercian churches in England. It is possible to get some idea of its area from the detached archway still standing on the road that leads to Oldstead.

An abbey was founded on this site only after much tribulation. The story is told by Philip, the third abbot, and is printed in Dugdale's *Monasticon* (v. 349). In 1134 twelve monks under their abbot, Gerald, were driven out of Furness Abbey by Scottish plunderers and fled towards York in a wagon drawn by eight oxen. There are two versions of what then happened, but somewhere in the neighbourhood of Thirsk they encountered the steward of Gundreda, the mother of Roger de Mowbray, who was still an infant. Gundreda sent the little band to interview her uncle (or nephew), Robert de Alnetto, who had been a monk at Whitby but was now living as a hermit at Hode. The hermit seems to have recommended Gerald to break with Furness, but for this purpose it was necessary to journey to Savigny in France to obtain permission from a chapter of the order. Gerald set off on this mission, but on his way back died at York. Meanwhile the monks had made the most of 'the cow pasture of Cambe' and other land in the neighbourhood of Hode, but their numbers had increased and they appealed to Gundreda and Mowbray to give them a site for a new monastery. The church and village of Byland were assigned to them—not the present Byland, but a village now called Old Byland which is only two miles up the dale from Rievaulx. (The Reverend W. Eastmead states that the name was originally La Bellalanda, or pleasant land; and why not if a hermit in the region could have a name like de Alnetto? Roger's name, too, was originally de Albini.) Here in 1143 they erected their first monastery, but alas, the sound of the bells of Rievaulx went up the dale and the sound of the bells of Byland went down the dale and the monks of both monasteries were distracted beyond endurance—'quod non dicebat nec diu potuit aliqualiter sustineri.' So four years later the newcomers reduced their holding to a grange and went over the hill to Oldstead (then called Stocking) and here they cleared a large tract of woodland and drained a marsh, and on the eve of All Saints, in the year 1177, they dedicated a new abbey to the Blessed Virgin, 'having a noble cathedral, and monastery, which continued in a flourishing condition till the general dissolution'.

Here, indeed, the Virgin may have presided over the building. The lancets that remain are slender, and there is a suggestion of grace and fantasy in the trefoil-headed doorways. It is significant, perhaps, that Laurence Sterne, who is the main subject of this chapter, associated the place with nuns. 'When I am at Coxwold in the summer,' he wrote to Eliza, his 'Brahmine' and last brief love, 'what a sweet companion will thy idea be unto me; and what new pleasures will it afford me when I go to visit my nuns! —I give this title to an afternoon pilgrimage I frequently make to the ruins of a Benedictine Monastery, about a mile and a half from my cottage.

'These remains are situated on the banks of a clear gliding stream; on the opposite side whereof rises a bold ridge of hills, thick with wood—and finely varied by jutting rocks and broken precipices; and these are so very abrupt, that they now not only by their magnitude, but by the shade they cast, increase the solemnity of the place.—Many parts of the ruin are still entire; the refectory is almost perfect, and a great part of the chapel has hitherto defied the power of time.—A few bunches of alders grow fantastically among the broken columns and contrast, with their verdure, the dark green ivy which clings to the walls.—But it is not all solitude and silence!—A few cottages are scattered here and there in the suburbs of this venerable pile, which has, I suppose, furnished the materials for erecting them.

'To this place, after my coffee, unless prevented by inclement skies, I guide my daily steps. The pathway leads, by a gentle descent, thro' many beautiful enclosures and embowering thickets, —which gradually prepare the mind for the deep impressions which this solemn place never fails to make on mine.—There I rest against a pillar till some affecting sentiment bring tears upon my cheek:—sometimes I sit me down upon a stone, and pluck up the weeds that grow about it,—then, perhaps, I lean over a neighbouring gate, and watch the gliding brook before me, and listen to its gentle murmurs; they are oftentimes in unison with my feelings. Here it is I catch those *sombre* tints of sentiment which I sometimes give to the world—to humanize and rob it of its spleen.'*

It is a self-indulgent picture, but essentially true to Sterne's character, and I would not need any other justification for my great devotion to his name and memory. The clear gliding stream he speaks of is probably the one now called the Long Beck; but the Holbeck, which glides at the end of my own field in Stonegrave, rises at the foot of that same bold ridge of hills; and I would only have to walk to the source of my beck to meet the gentle ghost of Yorick.

Such physical proximity would perhaps in any case have aroused my interest in Sterne's character and work, but I soon discovered some deeper spring of sympathy. I have already published two or three essays on Sterne, and do not wish on this occasion either to defend the character or praise the work: but I can perhaps explain the sympathy.

Even I would not maintain that Sterne was a typical Yorkshireman, but Sterne's father was the son of a county family which for several generations had had a small estate at Elvington six

---

* *Laurence Sterne, Second Journal to Eliza.* Hitherto known as *Letters Supposed to have been written by Yorick and Eliza* but now shown to be a later version of the *Journal to Eliza.* Transcribed from the copy in the British Museum and presented with an Introduction by Margaret R. B. Shaw. London (Bell), 1929.

Other quotations in this chapter are from the Shakespeare Head Edition of the Writings of Laurence Sterne, Oxford (Basil Blackwell), 1927. Cf. also *A Sentimental Journey.* By Laurence Sterne. Edited with an Introduction by Herbert Read. London (Scholartis Press), 1929.

miles east of York, and his great-grandfather, Richard Sterne, was Archbishop of York from 1664 to 1683, that is to say, in Thomas Comber's lifetime. Comber knew the Archbishop well, called him 'a pious, learned and grave man; a lover of scholars, prudent, and well skilled in the laws'. He died at the age of eighty-seven, still in office, and Comber was among those who carried him to his grave.

Sterne is something unique in English literature—a free spirit. It may be that the wandering existence he led as a child ensured that his heart, as he once expressed it, was not encompassed with adamant. His father, as a younger son, had decided on a military career, and as an ensign of the 34th Foot (a crack regiment) had gone to the wars in Flanders and there married the daughter-in-law of 'a noted sutler'. ('*N.B.* He was in debt to him.') The marriage was an unfortunate one and Sterne never knew a mother's affection. His father, whom he described as 'a little smart man—active to the last degree, in all exercises—most patient of fatigue and disappointments, of which it pleased God to give him full measure—he was in his temper somewhat rapid, and hasty—but of a kindly, sweet disposition, void of all design; and so innocent in his own intentions, that he suspected no one; so that you might have cheated him ten times a day, if nine had not been sufficient for your purpose'.

In the short 'memoirs' which he wrote for his daughter Lydia, from which I have taken the above description, Sterne gives us a dizzying list of the places to which his mother, as an officer's wife, was transported: Clonmel in Ireland (where Sterne was born in 1713), Elvington, Exeter, Dublin, the Isle of Wight, Wicklow, Dublin, Mullengar, Carrickfergus—all in ten years. Other children were born and (all but one) died. But from Carrickfergus at the age of ten, Laurence was sent to a school near Halifax.

It so happened that I, too, at the age of ten, and a hundred and eighty years later, was sent to a school near Halifax. It is a little uncertain whether Sterne's school was the Heath or the Hipperholme grammar school—possibly he divided his time between masters at both. My school did not exist then, but it lies between Heath and Hipperholme, and I was familiar with them both. This, however, is a trivial coincidence. My real links with Sterne are the villages and becks in which, unless prevented by inclement skies I too guide my daily steps. When I first read *Tristram*

Shandy I met the people that still, in my innocent days, lived about me.

That a regional novel should also be so universal is one of those natural paradoxes which I have attempted to explain elsewhere (though Coleridge had explained it before me). There is no philosophical problem, for humanity does not change from Ithaca to Yorkshire, from one millennium to another. The difficulty is to be human in literature, for literature is a convention and language itself a dark screen between our first impressions and our present memories. The miracle of Chaucer, Shakespeare and Sterne—and I put them on the same level in this respect—is that language with them is transparent—or, if that implies a lack of attention, which would be misleading, let me say translucent. Memory and meaning shine through the words without distortion, and this metaphor would serve for the sentiment, which is transmitted without loss of warmth.

I believe George Eliot once said that the people we most admire, whether in life or in literature, are not necessarily those most like ourselves. But equally we must not assume that an author is like his writing, and that Sterne therefore spent his life in unconstrained frivolity. He often describes himself as grave or serious, and Nollekens in his beautiful bust carved him thus. 'When I was a poor curate,' he told Eliza, 'and a poorer Vicar in Yorkshire, and confined by necessity to my cottage,—I cultivated, as far as the chill hand of poverty would let me, a little knowledge of painting and music; and was, really, a very tolerable proficient in both, considering my situation, and how unfavourable it was to such elegant attainments.' He was punctilious in the perform-ance of his duties to his parishioners, delivered better sermons than most vicars, and until fame came to him, lived modestly in his 'philosophical cottage'. Between his ministrations he would dig and root in his garden, fish for a trout, pick a dish of strawberries, and sit in the evening under his bower of honeysuckle. Occasion-ally—perhaps frequently in the season—he would ride into York to spend an evening in a coffee-house or at the Assembly Rooms; and sometimes he would go to Scarborough for his health. For complete relaxation he visited his Cambridge friend John Hall-Stevenson at Skelton Castle, near Saltburn, within a day's drive. At Crazy Castle, as Hall-Stevenson had renamed his seat, there was good fare and a well-kept cellar, and above all a finer library than Sterne could ever hope to possess. There were also, on occasion, the Demoniacs, a club of convivial spirits whom Hall-Stevenson entertained every October—'a jollier set never met, either before or since the flood'. Sterne, who was called the Blackbird on account of his clerical dress, entertained them with his fiddle, which he played reasonably well.

Sterne discovered his talent for writing late in his short life—the first volumes of *Tristram Shandy* were published on January 1, 1760, and he died eight years later (on March 18, 1768), a month after the publication of *A Sentimental Journey*. He burnt himself out in these last few years, and his character may have suffered under the ordeal. It was a sudden glory, and he would have been the last to complain. But this is not the Sterne I think of, as I rest against a pillar at Byland or pass through Coxwold or Sutton. I think of the first forty-seven years of his life, before the world outside Yorkshire united to destroy the man who called himself Yorick.

Yorick is a sentimental name for a sentimental man, but it was well chosen, as was Shandy for his house—a Yorkshire dialect word meaning crazy. Shakespeare's Yorick, was 'a fellow of infinite jest, of most excellent fancy', but his name, to Hamlet, was a *memento mori*, 'and now how abhorred in my imagination it is!' This sinister undertone may not be present in *Tristram Shandy*, but the figure he depicts in *Tristram Shandy* has its shadow:

'. . . instead of that cold phlegm and exact regularity of sense and humours, you would have look'd for, in one so extracted;— he was, on the contrary, as mercurial and sublimated a composition,—as heteroclite a creature in all his declensions;—with as much life and whim, and *gaîté de coeur* about him, as the kindliest climate could have engendered and put together. With all this sail, poor *Yorick* carried not one ounce of ballast; he was utterly unpractised in the world; and, at the age of twenty-six, knew just about as well how to steer his course in it, as a romping, unsuspicious girl of thirteen: So that upon his first setting out, the brisk gale of his spirits, as you will imagine, ran him foul ten times in a day of some body's tackling; and as the grave and more slow-paced were oftenest in his way,—you may likewise imagine, 'twas with such he had generally the ill-luck to get most entangled. For aught I know, there might be some mixture of unlucky wit at the bottom of such *Fracas*:—For, to speak the truth, *Yorick* had an invincible dislike and opposition of his nature to gravity;—not to gravity as such;—for where gravity was wanted, he would be the most grave or serious of mortal men for days and weeks together;—but he was an enemy to the affectation of it, and declared open war against it, only as it appeared a cloak for ignorance, or for folly; and then, whenever it fell in his way, however sheltered and protected, he seldom gave it much quarter.'

And then, after declaring that the very essence of gravity is design, and consequently deceit, there follows Sterne's rendering of Rochefoucauld's definition of it: *A mysterious carriage of the body to cover the defects of the mind.*

We know that Keats was familiar with *Tristram Shandy*, and it may be that his notion of *Negative Capability* ('which Shakespeare possessed so enormously') owes something to Sterne's character of Yorick—in any case, Sterne was certainly also 'a man . . . capable of being in uncertainties, Mysteries, doubts, without any irritable reaching after fact and reason'. It is usual to call his philosophy Shandeism, but there is nothing crazy about it and perhaps Yorickism would be a better word. Bagehot, in his essay on Sterne, asserts bluntly, 'Sterne was a pagan'—which does not alarm me. Bagehot does not tell us what a pagan is, save that he leads an easy life, but he tells us that Sterne was a great author because of his wonderful sympathy with, and wonderful power of, representing simple human nature. 'He excels, perhaps, all other writers in mere simple description of common sensitive human action. He places before you in their simplest form the elemental facts of human life; he does not view them through the intellect, he scarcely views them through the imagination; he does but reflect the unimpaired impression which the facts of life, which does not change from age to age, make on the deep basis of human feeling, which changes as little though years go on . . . His mind was like a pure lake of delicate water: it reflects the ordinary landscape, the rugged hills, the loose pebbles, the knotted and the distorted firs perfectly and as they are, yet with a charm and fascination that they have not in themselves.'*

This is well said, and yet I do not feel it is the whole truth, and it would seem to contradict one of Bagehot's criticisms of

---

* Walter Bagehot's essay on 'Sterne and Thackeray' was written in 1864 and reprinted in *Literary Studies*, 1879.

Sterne—that he was *provincial*—'redolent of an inferior society'. I don't know what superior society Bagehot was thinking of— perhaps that of Lombard Street. For how can the elemental facts of human life, which do not change from age to age, and are impressed on the deep basis of human feeling, be at the same time barbarous, inferior, provincial? Sterne admittedly has not the myriad mind of Shakespeare, but his Uncle Toby is of the same stuff and stature as Falstaff, and Yorick himself is a Hamlet of the Enlightenment. We must not make the mistake of giving Sterne a mysterious carriage of the body, but he himself once confessed (to Jean Baptiste Suard) that he owed everything (beyond his natural endowments and the daily reading of the Old and New Testaments) to a prolonged study of Locke 'which he had begun in youth and continued through life'; and it is quite true, as he then said, that anyone acquainted with Locke might discover his hand 'in all his pages, in all his lines, in all his expressions . . . (Locke's philosophy) is a philosophy which never attempts to explain the miracle of sensation; but reverently leaving the miracle in the hands of God, it unfolds all the secrets of the mind; and shunning the errors to which other theories of knowledge are exposed, it arrives at all truths accessible to the understanding'.

'The miracle of sensation'—there again is a phrase that binds Sterne to Keats ('O for a life of Sensations rather than of Thoughts') and points to the nature of his pagan philosophy and the pellucid quality of his art. In this respect Sterne is central to the whole of the English Romantic tradition, as I have traced it in *The True Voice of Feeling*, and this more than anything else probably explains the attraction he has for me as a writer. But it was not my intention to discuss the writer, but rather the man and his associations with my native background.

In spite of the sudden glory of the last years of his life, Sterne died a poor man, and the auction of all the household goods and furniture from Shandy Hall was a pathetic occasion. The lots included a cow, 'a parcel of hay, a handsome post-chaise with a pair of exceeding good horses, and a compleat set of coloured table-china'. His books went for £80, and his personal effects altogether realized £400, but his debts amounted to £1,100. A scramble for his literary remains took place in the ensuing years; they were submitted to a process of vamping by his widow and an unscrupulous hack called William Combe (of Dr. Syntax fame) with the result that what is genuine among them has now to be detected by a stylistic divining rod.

I have said nothing of Sterne's domestic life, which was unhappy; nor of the solace he received from several romantic friendships with young ladies. There is no evidence to suggest that he was vicious, though he was undoubtedly, even unconcernedly, unwise. I like to think of his life at Coxwold as he described it to Eliza, the last of his loves:

'O tis a delicious retreat! both from its beauty & air of Solitude, & so sweetly does everything about it invite your mind to rest from its labours and be at peace with itself & the world—That tis the only place Eliza I could live in at this juncture—I hope one day you will like it as much as your Bramin—It shall be decorated & made worthy of you by the time Fate encourages me to look for you—I have made you a sweet sitting-room (as I told you) already—& am projecting a good bed-chamber adjoining it, with a pretty Dressing-room for You which connects them together—& when they are finished will be as sweet a set of romantic apartments, as you ever beheld—the sleeping room will be very large—the dressing room thro which you pass into your Temple will be little—but big enough to hold a Dressing Table, a couple of chairs, with room for your Nymph to stand at her ease both behind and on either side of you—with spare room to hang a dozen petticoats, gowns, etc.—& shelves for as many Bandboxes—Your little Temple I have described—& what will it hold—but if it ever holds You and I, my Eliza—the room will not be too little for us—but we shall be *too big* for the Room.—'

And three days later: '*I wish I was in Arno's Vale!*—But I am in the Vale of Coxwold & wish you saw how princely a manner I live in it—tis a land of Plenty—I sit down alone to Venison, fish or wild foul, or a couple of fowls—with curds & strawberries & cream and all the simple clean plenty which a rich valley can produce—with a Bottle of wine at my right hand (as in Bond Street) to drink your health—I have a hundred hens & chickens about my yard—& not a parishioner catches a hare a rabbit or a trout but he brings it as an offering—In short tis a golden valley—and will be the golden age when you govern the rural feast my Bramine, & are the Mistress of my table, & spread it with elegancy and that natural grace & bounty with which heaven has distinguished You . . . Time goes on slowly—every thing stands still

–hours seem days & days seem years whilst you lengthen the distance between us–from Madras to Bombay–I shall think it shortening–and then desire & expectation will be upon the rack again–Come–Come–'

But the Bramine never came. Sterne had met her first in January 1767; she was the wife of a merchant in India and she left for that country in April of the same year. Within a year, having meanwhile written the Journal to Eliza and *A Sentimental Journey*, Sterne died alone in his Bond Street lodgings in London. He was buried in the burial-ground belonging to St. George's Church, Hanover Square, which was along the Bayswater Road. A legend subsequently spread that the resurrection men stole his body to sell for dissection and that his bones finally came to rest in the Anatomical Museum at Cambridge. Sterne would not have cared greatly: he may often have meditated on the bones of Cromwell, whose body had been snatched by a trick from the executioner when it was ordered to be exposed at Tyburn, and secretly interred by his daughter in Newburgh Priory, half a mile from Shandy Hall. Yorick was his chosen name, and he knew to what base our bodies return. 'Alexander died, Alexander was buried, Alexander returned to dust, the dust is earth, of earth we make loam, and why of that loam whereto he was converted might they not stop a beer-barrel?'

Shandy Hall is now a private farm-house and I should doing its worthy tenants a bad service if inadvertently I encouraged anyone to visit it. But it is much as it was in Sterne's days, and still retains the ingenious system by means of which an air duct at the side of the large open fireplace in his study conveyed the warm air to his bed-chamber above. It is not a large house–a 'philosophical cottage'–but an immortal 'fragment of life' was conceived here, and since there is no plain marble slab to mark a grave in the near-by churchyard, 'tis here that the passenger going by should stop to cast a look upon the only material memorial to Sterne's goast that exists–signing, as he walks on,

Alas! Poor YORICK!

6

The Mill at the World's End

As soon as I was once more established among the scenes of my childhood, I decided to revisit Bransdale, that oasis on the Moors which I have described in 'The Innocent Eye'. It is no longer inaccessible: the road from Kirbymoorside has been metalled and fettled and carries one over the shoulder of Rudland Rigg to the head of the dale, which is strangely called Cockayne. One can even continue past the shooting lodge and then diagonally up the dale side and over Pockley Moor and the head of Riccal Dale to Helmsley, the whole circuit from Stonegrave amounting to little more than thirty miles.

But that is not the way I prefer to visit Bransdale. It is now even more difficult than in my childhood to make one's way on foot through Kirkdale Woods, and along Hodge Beck. The slopes of the river bank are sometimes precipitous, and one must cross and re-cross the rocky bed of the stream many times. There are two or three oases in the dale, the first after Kirkdale being Hold Cauldron, a mill formerly kept by one of my grandfather's brothers; but these small isolated mills were gradually put out of business by improvements in machinery and transport, and I think my great-uncle must have been the last of the millers—he went to America: the millhouse is now a small farm, and chickens roost among the rusty wheels.

At the head of Bransdale, now difficult to discover because the track to it is overgrown, is another deserted mill, and this too once belonged to an ancestor of mine, but on my mother's side of the family—his name, like that of my grandfather, was William Strickland. An inscription on the face of the mill tells us that W.S. rebuilt it in 1812. There are other inscriptions on the walls of the house, still precise after more than a century. Over the lintel of a door William carved the admonition REMEMBER THY END and the date A.D. 1817, and beyond the immediate precincts of the mill, at the edge of the moor, he erected a sun-dial and on this carved the mottoes *Quod hora est vide* and *Time and Life move swiftly.* The date on the sun-dial is 1819, but William added the year from the creation of the world, A.D. 5824.

On the western wall of the house William's son Emmanuel (also the name of one of my grandfather's sons) carved Hebrew and Greek texts, and beneath them recorded in Latin that this was done 'per me E^l Strickland, B.A. Coll. Reg. Cantab. et Sacerdotem Vicarium, Ingleby Greenhow, Cleveland, 1837'. Ingleby Greenhow lies on the northern edge of the moors, about six miles across the bleak hump of Cockayne Rigg. The sources of Hodge Beck, which turned the miller's wheel in Bransdale, are but a few hundred yards from the sources of the beck that runs past the vicarage in Ingleby Greenhow.

The records at Ingleby show that Emmanuel served as a curate there in 1835 and again in 1837, but a certain John Dixon was vicar in these years, which suggests that the son went on living at the mill after the father's death. These vain inscriptions are the only memorials of a family that has vanished from the scene. The stone was well cut and the lettering is still clear, but no one now visits this forlorn ruin. In winter the sheep and shaggy moorland cattle shelter against the sturdy walls, but the windows are all broken and the loosened tiles slither one by one into the beck. Time and life stand still.

I have often thought of seeking permission to rebuild the house so that I might retire to this idyllic spot, but such intentions always seem to conflict with inescapable duties, and there is one sufficient deterrent. It is said that some years ago a cloudburst at the head of the dale caused a sudden downpour, which rushing down the steep slopes, overwhelmed the mill-dam and flooded the little oasis. Elaborate precautions would have to be taken to safeguard against a similar disaster.

If I have not moved bodily to Bransdale, I have often been there in spirit—it is my spiritual hermitage, the 'bright jewel' to which I often retire in moods of despair. But who was Bran, and what do the place names in this little oasis signify—Clegret, Groat, Yoad, Smout, Breck, Wath, Urra and Hagg? I am no philologist,

but they sound to me like Norse names, and all Norse names are
an archetypal music to my ears:

> *beck, dale and gill*
> *garth, force and fell*
> *holm, lund and keld*
> *ness, scar and tarn*
> *scale, thorpe and toft*
> *thwaite, with and wath*

The Vikings came to England in the eighth century, sacked
Lindisfarne in 793 (which it is hard to forgive them), devastated
Jarrow in 794, and no doubt moved inland from these beach-heads.
They went further—to Western Scotland and Ireland, to the
Orkneys and Man, to Normandy, Russia, Iceland. They took
prisoners in Morocco (they called them 'Blue-men') and raided
Provence. They sailed to Italy and captured Pisa and threatened
Rome. In some places they stayed, or left settlements, and this
north-east corner of Yorkshire seems to have been one of them.
Why they should have left a settlement in this moorland oasis of
Bransdale is more than I can say—perhaps they were driven into
it as a redoubt by subsequent invaders—by the Normans who
ravaged Yorkshire in 1068. But for ten centuries, in which peace
has been more devastating than war, they have retained, not only
their place-names, but a sense of belonging to their homesteads.
There has been more weakening of that sense in the past fifty
years than during the preceding millennium: what William the
Conqueror could not obliterate has crumbled under the relentless
pressure of economic laws. Those silent and deserted farmsteads
are there to bear witness. I wrote *Moon's Farm* as an elegy for this
waste land.

These moorland dales—the upper reaches of Ryedale, Bilsdale,
Bransdale, Farndale and Rosedale—are still to me the most
romantic and least desecrated landscapes in England, but not for
long. All this region is now a National Park, which means that
it will swiftly become a parking lot for caravans and coaches.
Their season may be short, and the rarest beauty of the dales is in
early spring or late autumn—even in winter they have the wistful
beauty of sleeping children. That is a pathetic fallacy, no doubt,
but there is a valid association of landscape and body-images as
certain sculptors have realized (above all, the Yorkshireman

Henry Moore), and these particular moors and dales are not black and rugged, like Emily Brontë's moors in the West Riding, but sinuous and pearly, their contours as smooth as youthful limbs, their languour never drooping into slackness or dullness, but always infinitely still.

> *A distant, dreamy, dim blue chain*
> *Of mountains circling every side;*
> *A heaven so clear, an earth so calm,*
> *So sweet, so soft, so hushed an air;*
> *And deepening still the dream-like charm,*
> *Wild moor-sheep feeding everywhere.*

That, in its gentleness, will serve for the Cleveland moors, but there enters into Emily's verses notes of wildness that are too violent:

> *Awaken, o'er all my dear moorland,*
> *West-wind, in thy glory and pride!*
> *Oh! call me from valley and lowland,*
> *To walk by the hill-torrent's side!*
>
> *It is swelled with the first snowy weather;*
> *The rocks they are icy and hoar,*
> *And sullenly waves the long heather,*
> *And the fern-leaves are sunny no more.*
>
> *There are no yellow stars on the mountains;*
> *The bluebells have long died away*
> *From the brink of the moss-bedded fountain—*
> *From the side of the wintry brae.*
>
> *But lovelier than cornfields all waving*
> *In emerald, and vermeil, and gold,*
> *Are the heights where the north-wind is raving,*
> *And the crags where I wandered of old.*

There are no crags on my moors, and no wuthering winds, but the spirit of the moors that pervades Emily's poetry has always been in my own blood, and I am never wholly myself unless they are a background to my thoughts. As I return from York and reach the ridge of the Howardian Hills above Hovingham, and see the misty-blue circuit around me as far as the eye can reach, I cry with Emily:

A DEARTH OF WILD FLOWERS

For the moors! For the moors, where the short grass
Like velvet beneath us should lie!
For the moors! For the moors, where each high pass
Rose sunny against the clear sky!

For the moors, where the linnet was trilling
Its song on the old granite stone;
Where the lark: the wild skylark: was filling
Every breast with delight like its own!

But what, asks Emily in another, perhaps her greatest poem,
have these lonely 'mountains' worth revealing? And she answers:

More glory and more grief than I can tell:
The earth that wakes one human heart to feeling
Can centre both the worlds of Heaven and Hell.

A pantheistic notion, no doubt; but a landscape in which we
are born and to which we must always return for the release of the
tensions born in exile, has this mysterious power of reconciliation,
of absolution. That is one of the truths neglected by the modern
world, and in any case there are now too many alienated souls to
make a universal centring of Heaven and Hell possible. But the
need for roots exists: the need which unappeased drives the human
heart to paralysis and self-destruction.

7

A Dearth of Wild Flowers

David Thoreau held that it requires a direct dispensation
from Heaven to become a walker, and I believe him:
ambulator nascitur, non fit. I walk as naturally as I breathe,
or perform any other bodily function: to exist is to walk, to
assert freedom of bodily movement. And this freedom is basic to
all other freedoms—there is no progress in my thoughts unless
they are geared to a slowly changing landscape. Some of the
Greek philosophers rightly associated thought with walking, and
were for that reason called peripatetic. But walking in our time,
like philosophy in our time, has declined to a state of paralysis.
I live in the deep country, yet apart from an occasional game-
keeper or a gipsy poaching, I do not remember in the past ten
years meeting another walker. The paths across the fields have
long since been ploughed away; even bridle-paths which in my
childhood were busy with human traffic have completely dis-
appeared.

Two causes have contributed to this rapid obliteration of path-
ways: the internal combustion engine and the decline in church-
going. Many of the old footpaths radiated from the church, and
one of the pleasantest scenes of the age of faith was to see the little
groups of people in their Sunday clothes, carrying prayer books
and parasols, converging on the village church from distant farms
and cottages. Nowadays, if they ever come to church, they may
walk along the village street for a few yards, but from any dis-
tance more than half a mile they will come in a car or a bus. In
some parishes elaborate schemes for picking up the faithful exist:
faith now moves on wheels.

And so does labour. The farm-hand has become a tractor-
driver, and keeps to the roads. He will take a tractor half a mile to

pick up an empty sack or a discarded coat. He travels to his work or from his work in a bus or on a motor cycle. Walking he regards as a waste of time and energy, and since his work is arduous, one cannot blame him. He has more excuse than the townsman who sits in an office all day and in a car all the weekend.

The obliteration of footpaths has forcibly restricted the range of the walker, but luckily there still exist deserted woodland paths, and the dales and the moors. Even in such places the solitary walker is not encouraged: he is suspected of breaking down fences or of disturbing the pheasants. He has lost the footpaths that were his legal ground, and must now be suspected as a poacher. But if he uses his discretion, and knows when to keep his dog to heel, he may still be tolerated. There is a legal provision, which I have never had to exercise, to the effect that an immediate offer of a shilling to pay for any damage you may be accused of causing, protects you from eviction and wilful prosecution. It is better to be on friendly terms with the farmers and landlords: to be accepted as a familiar figure in the local landscape.

In what consists the pleasure of walking? Partly, of course, the gentle well-being induced by such an exercise of limbs and body. Essentially, however, the experience is a stimulus to one's thoughts, a calming of one's nerves. The stimulus comes from external things—the texture of the ground, the weather in the sky, the contours of the hills, the infinite patterns of the trees. Calm follows from the gentle rhythmic movement of the body.

I may go the same walk a hundred times in a year, but it is never the same experience. The weather is never the same, the light and temperature change, the birds have a different behaviour, the cattle have moved into a different field and assumed a different grouping. But most of all the textures have changed—the textures of the grasses and the hedges, of the trees and the stones. What infinite variety there is in the colour of bark from day to day, from hour to hour, even in one tree: and how the grass changes its texture beneath the plodding feet! More rarely one may experience the exquisite sensation of walking over the crisp surface of frozen stubble. Ditches are an endless delight: their ruddy beds where crystal-clear water trickles slowly, the ferns and flowers that spring from their spongy banks. Hedges of fantastic intricacy: some tortured by man into tidiness, others agonized by the raving winds. There are thorns of great antiquity, their boles and branches twisted like Laocoon's family, with hollows full of the berries the wild birds have hoarded.

But rich as these delights may be, they are not so various as they were fifty years ago. The animals are scarcer—myxomatosis has cleared the land of the rabbit, a pest well lost, however much he may have added to the interest of a walk. He may have had some part to play in the economy of nature—he certainly helped to keep the man-made footpaths cropped—but I will not attempt to make out a case in his defence. The hare is immune, and may have increased in numbers. Occasionally I surprise a young family at play. More rarely I see a fox or a stoat, but I am not abroad long enough nor range far enough to make such chances frequent. In general, in a landscape in which even the horse is now a rarity, the animal life of the countryside is much poorer than it used to be.

I have never mastered the migration of birds, and at any time of the year hardly know what to expect. A few herons nest above Gilling and I know a marsh along the banks of the Rye where I can occasionally surprise them. More rarely still a buzzard flaps heavily away from my path. Partridges and pheasants abound, and one can never sufficiently wonder at the Oriental splendour of the cock pheasant, a legendary bird brought to England by the Romans. The Romans said the Argonauts brought it into Europe, but the ornithologists believe it to have been indigenous.

There is more than one variety of pheasant: the *P. Colchicus*, the common pheasant, which is said to have come from the River Phasis in Colchis; the Chinese or ring-necked pheasant; the Japanese or green pheasant—but all these species interbreed and perhaps the commonest of them all is a hybrid. I have seen a white pheasant but whether it was an albino or the rare snow-pheasant (if that is white) I do not know. I heard a raucous squawking in the field below my house and approaching saw half a dozen pheasants fluttering in and out of the branches of the trees and occasionally swooping down to the ground. I then noticed a movement low in the grass and coming nearer saw a white bird ducking as if to hide itself. It rose as I got nearer and I then saw that it was a white cock pheasant: it flew off pursued by the others. I can only suppose that its oddity made it an object of suspicion to the conventional pheasant: an instinctive reaction not unknown to the human species.

The greatest deprivation suffered by the solitary walker is among the flora rather than the fauna of the countryside. The memory-images from childhood are too precise to be deceptive. The common cornfields were bright with red poppies and blue cornflowers; speedwell and pimpernel carpeted the arable land and the pastures in spring would be ablaze with buttercups. All these have vanished, victims to the selective weed-killers that science has perfected. Some weeds seem to be indestructible, but they are the dull ones—thistles and dandelions. Grasses, too, seem to have been 'standardized'; that extraordinary sense of 'bounteous' or 'pied' meadows that one finds in Spenser and Milton, indeed, in all English lyrical poetry, is no longer there. Grovelets of wild roses still flourish, and there is the annual miracle of the hawthorn hedges which lace all England with delight; but everywhere else there is a dearth of wild flowers.

All modern developments—weed-killers, motor-cars, tractors, mechanization, tourism, the radio, the cinema, urbanization (words as ugly as the things they signify)—have combined to destroy the countryside that was evident to my innocent eye. There are improvements—in housing, in health services, in education—but the price that has been paid for them is not only the destruction of a society that may have been insufferably patriarchal, but the end of a way of life out of which whatever poetry and intelligence we possess arose as naturally as poppies and cornflowers from the undisciplined earth. It has often been remarked how much of the genius of England is associated with the country house, particularly the parsonage. It is no less evident how much delinquency and crime are associated with the modern city. It may not be the city as such that breeds such a contrast: it is more likely to be the alienation of sensibility that is the inevitable consequence of mechanization. It is as simple as that: we have lost touch with *things*, lost the physical experience that comes from a direct contact with the organic processes of nature. The man who followed the plough felt a tremor conducted from the shining thrust of the coulter in the earth along his arms and into his heart. To dig, to harrow, to sow; to weed, to prune, to scythe; to walk, to ride, to swim; to watch the birth and death of animals; to be conscious of defecation and slow decay, bloom and rot; to participate with all one's senses in the magical rhythm of the seasons—all these are such elementally human experiences that to be deprived of them is to become something less than human. There has never been and never can be a civilization that is not rooted in such organic processes. We know it—instinctively we know it —and walk like blind animals into a darker age than history has ever known.

8

The Adamantine Sickle

And having received also from Hermes an adamantine
sickle he flew to the ocean and caught the Gorgons asleep.
APOLLODORUS, II, iv. 2.

I

The reader who has followed my narrative thus far will perhaps have been left with the impression that I have taken him to three or four halting-places and given no hint of a final destination. More than once I have emphasized the fact that I do not consider even the ordinary process of education at an end; my intellectual curiosity remains insatiable. But the mere acquisition of knowledge has never been my aim—otherwise I could so easily have become an academic scholar or an archaeologist. I am only interested in facts that feed an interest which is total, directed to the universe and to life as an existing whole; and it is my intuition of the nature of that wholeness, my desire to hold it within my mind as a coherent conception, which drives me on to the discovery of facts and their reconciliation in a philosophy of life. In a sense I am a solipsist: that is to say, I believe that the world I discover, as well as the philosophical interpretation I give to it, is contained within myself, and inevitably conditioned by my temperament. Nietzsche's command: Become what thou art, seems to me to be an improvement even on the Delphic oracle. Thus, so long as I remain true to that command, I find myself continually returning to certain fundamental beliefs or attitudes which have their unity or reconciliation in my personality. In this final chapter I shall try to describe them.

If I begin with aesthetics, it is because I have accumulated most evidence of this kind, and found it a sufficient basis for a general philosophy. I do my ideas too much honour by calling them a philosophy, and it seems doubtful if I shall ever have the time or leisure to elaborate them even into the outline of a philosophical system. But such as they are, these ideas are universal in their implications, and referable to other lives than mine.

My profoundest experience has been, not religious, nor moral, but aesthetic: certain moments of creative activity and, less intense but more frequent, certain moments of sensibility in the presence of works of art. The very vividness of this kind of experience led me to wonder about its nature and to inquire into its place in the universal scheme of things. It gradually became clear to me that the aesthetic experience was not a superficial phenomenon, an expression of surplus energy, a secondary feature of any kind, but rather something related to the very structure of the universe. The more we analyse a work of art, whether it be architecture, painting, poetry or music, the more evident it becomes that it has an underlying structure; and when reduced to abstract terms, the laws of such a structure are the same whatever the kind of art— so that terms such as 'rhythm', 'balance' and 'proportion' can be used interchangeably in all the arts.

It was a short and obvious step to recognize at least an analogy and possibly some more direct relation, between such a mor-phology of art and the morphology of nature. I began to seek for more exact correspondences, first by making myself familiar with the conclusions reached by modern physicists about the structure of matter, and then by exploring the quite extensive literature on the morphology of art. Certain correspondences are easily estab-lished—the prevalence, for example, in art and in both organic and inorganic matter of the proportion known as the Golden Section. In the course of my research I naturally came across D'Arcy Thompson's *Growth and Form*, and this book, by showing that certain fundamental physical laws determine even the appar-ently irregular forms assumed by organic growth, enormously extended the analogy between art and nature. All this was a question of exact measurements and demonstrable equations, and merely gave a contemporary scientific sanction to the intuitions of Pythagoras and Plato, who centuries ago had found in *number* the clue to both the nature of the universe and the definition of beauty. Modern physicists, I found, might express themselves much more obscurely, but their implications were the same. In 1922 I found every confirmation I needed in Whitehead's *Principles of Natural Knowledge*, and I noted with zeal passages such as the following: 'Life is complex in its expression, involving more than percipience, namely desire, emotion, will, and feeling. It exhibits variations of grade, higher and lower, such that the higher grade presupposes the lower for its very existence. *This suggests a close identification of rhythm as the causal counterpart of life; namely, that wherever there is some rhythm there is some life, only perceptible to us when the analogies are sufficiently close.* The rhythm is then the life, in the sense in which it can be said to be included within nature.' There are other passages in this book which might, without any violence, be transposed from a work on physics to one on aesthetics. Here is one more example: 'A rhythm involves a pattern and to that extent is always self-identical. But no rhythm can be a mere pattern; for the rhythmic quality depends equally upon the differences involved in each exhibition of the pattern. The essence of rhythm is the fusion of sameness and novelty; so that the whole never loses the essential unity of the pattern, while the parts exhibit the contrast arising from the novelty of their detail. A mere recurrence kills rhythm as surely as does a mere confusion of differences. A crystal lacks rhythm from excess of pattern, while a fog is unrhythmic in that it exhibits a patternless confusion of detail.'

The analogy, particularly with the qualification implied in this second passage quoted from Whitehead, would account for the formal appeal of a large part of the world's art. But the more I thought of it, the more I became convinced that it would not include everything; and the part that was excluded was the part in which I was especially interested—romantic art. At one time I was tempted to find the distinction between classic and romantic art precisely in this difference: that the one observed the formal laws inherent in the structure of nature, whilst the other ignored them for the sake of some other values. But I think it has now been convincingly demonstrated (at least, in such test cases as the Parthenon) that even in its most pure and formal manifestations, classic art intuitively avoids an *exact* observation of the laws of natural morphology. It comes very near to them, and then, as if to assert the freedom of the artist's will, narrowly avoids them.

ADAMANTINE SICKLE

In romantic art, however, there is no such flirtation. Certain laws, of proportion and rhythm, are observed in all but the most anarchic types of expressionism; but having gone so far on the basis of such laws, the work of art then seems to take a leap into the unknown. The laws themselves are contradicted, or are entirely disregarded; and a new reality is created, requiring a sudden passage from perception to intuition, and carrying with it a heightened mode of consciousness.

The analogy for this transition was ready waiting in the new quantum theory. But to pursue this analogy, even granted that the quantum theory itself had been definitely established, would have been too delicate and difficult a task. I was content with the fact that physics had apparently provided an escape from a situation that threatened to be wholly mechanistic. If all art could be referred to natural laws, to a system of numerical proportions, then evidently we were within reach of tests and measurements—in short, of academic rules which meant an end to all creative originality (in the Bergsonian sense) and therefore to all artistic evolution. But though physics might still have its problems to solve, and though the universe was far from being mapped out in its entirety, my analogical excursions had convinced me that a profound relation exists between the reality of art and the reality of nature—a conviction which Whitehead, approaching from the opposite direction, had also reached.

In short, the aesthetic view of life, which Kierkegaard had perceived as a possibility, had become much more realistic and practical, and I began to consider how far it would carry one in the conduct of life.

In the sphere of morals there did not seem to be any difficulty. Having rejected any code of morality dependent on a super-natural sanction, the only alternatives seemed to be, either an egoism as extreme as Max Stirner's, or a social code determined by the needs and guaranteed by the laws of the community of which one was a member. This latter solution was too relative and too pragmatic for my taste; and fundamentally I had no belief in social sanctions of any kind—they are only an excuse for tyranny. I therefore fell back upon some form of egoism, but though I recognized the logicality of the extremist position, and its freedom (Stirner took his motto from Goethe: 'Ich hab' mein' Sach' auf Nichts gestellt'), I was not prepared for its consequences, which seemed to me to involve hedonism (a life of unrestricted sensuousness, which always ends in despair) rather than a desirable eudemonism (a life of ordered goodness). But it gradually occurred to me that the principles I was working out in the aesthetic sphere could, as Plato had already suggested, be carried over into the ethical sphere, and that a valid analogy exists between the order of the universe, the order of art and the order of conduct. Goodness is living beauty—life ordered on the same principles of rhythm and harmony that are implicit in a work of art. Vulgarity is the only sin, in life as in art. The only danger of such a code was that it might lead to a priggish conformity or preciousness; but here again the analogy of the quantum theory came to my aid. At certain moments the individual is carried beyond his rational self, on to another ethical plane, where his actions are judged by new standards. The impulse which moves him to irrational action I have called the sense of glory, a phrase which is sometimes misunderstood, but which I find too appropriate to abandon. Related to this concept of glory is the concept of honour, which is the personal aspect of the sense of glory and a modest restraint on its expression—'L'honneur, c'est la pudeur virile', wrote De Vigny. No considerations of utility or expediency can explain the actions of men who at the inspired moment will throw away life itself to achieve their glory or to safeguard their honour; but without these concepts, life is reduced to a routine and cautious existence only worthy of meaner animals.

Admittedly such a morality has its dangers, and may be used in self-justification by any lunatic with a lust for power. But lunatics are a product of a diseased society, and I do not accept the gloomy doctrine that society is necessarily diseased. The impulse to depart from normal standards of the good and the beautiful usually arises from the felt need of new and higher standards. If it is asked who is to be judge of this need, then the answer is: the artist—the artist in that broad but special sense which includes all men who are capable of acts of creative originality, of instants of intuitive understanding of the nature of reality. An artist in relation to morals is more commonly known as a mystic, and it is sometimes very difficult to say where the poet ends and the mystic begins (I have already mentioned St. Theresa and St. John of the Cross, and Blake is the best English example).

To what extent these doctrines are supported by modern

psychology is perhaps a matter of opinion: to some extent it will depend on the interpretation we give to the findings of that science. But the moment of creative inspiration, whether it takes place on the plane of ethics or of art, is dynamic: it is caused by the sudden release of some kind of energy, and the only energy in question is psychic energy. I have put forward my own hypothesis in *Art and Society* (Chapter V), and it fits in with Freud's anatomy of the mental personality. It is only necessary to say here that this hypothesis accounts, not merely for the source of the energy underlying the phenomenon of inspiration, but also for the formal unity and ideological significance given to the verbal or plastic expression of such inspiration.

It was on the basis of this philosophy of art that I gave my support to that movement in contemporary art known as Surrealism. Some of my friends and critics, recognizing the reasonableness of my general attitude, have accused me of inconsistency —of 'flirting with the disreputable muse of Surrealism'. Whether what I mean by Surrealism corresponds to what that word means to its foremost French exponents is perhaps not certain: my interpretation is probably much wider. I have always regarded Surrealism as a first step towards a revindication and re-integration of the romantic tradition. Surrealism has developed various experimental methods: automatic writing, psychopathic simulation, 'paranoiac criticism'; but the means must not be confused with the end, which is nothing less than the application of the dialectical method to the problems of art, leading to a new synthesis of reality and unreality, of reason and unreason, of reflection and impulse. The laws which govern material reality, and which are the conscious or unconscious basis of a rational art, only carry us to the threshold of another order of reality, to which the dream is our main clue. 'It is only at the approach of the fantastic,' André Breton has said, 'at a point where human reason loses its control, that the most profound emotion of the individual has the fullest opportunity to express itself.' More than two thousand years ago Plato made much the same observation, in that immortal passage in *Ion* which concludes: 'For the poet is a light and winged and holy thing, and there is no invention in him until he has been inspired and is out of his senses, and the mind is no longer in him: when he has not attained to this state, he is powerless and is unable to utter his oracles.'

II

A unity of the aesthetic and the moral should logically include the practical, for this philosophy of mine though general is not abstract or idealistic, but in the proper sense of the word, existential. It is made actual in deeds: in the deed which is the work of art, in the deed which is an inspired moral act. In this sphere again I have been led by logic and by history to the adoption of what is commonly regarded as an irrational doctrine: anarchism. I have written a separate book on this subject (*Anarchy and Order*) and here I intend to do no more than show the relation of this political doctrine to the general philosophy of life which I am now attempting to outline.

Anarchism, by its more philosophical exponents, has always been advocated as the *natural* order of society. But this ideal may be interpreted in more ways than one. An anarchist like Thoreau interprets it in a regressive sense. Mankind is one of the species that have to live on the products of the earth, and as a consequence we are intimately bound to that earth. We break the bond at our peril. Modern industrial civilization has broken the bond and we are therefore miserable and unhealthy. We must abandon such an artificial mode of life and return to the fields and the woods to live in direct contact with the soil from which we derive our spiritual no less than our bodily sustenance.

This doctrine is a literal interpretation of natural laws and might be best called 'naturism'. I do not dismiss it entirely: it expresses a fundamental law, one which we must take into account. But man, by virtue of his consciousness and intellect, has raised himself on to a plane higher than that of animal existence. He has elaborated his life in many directions; and these elaborations, which include his aesthetic perceptions and enjoyments, demand a mode of life which is correspondingly complicated. The highest achievements of humanity—a Greek tragedy, a Beethoven symphony, a novel by Flaubert or Henry James—are an expression of this complication and can only be appreciated fully in a highly civilized environment.

It is the quality of this civilization that we must control. The fact that we have not controlled it, by any universal standard, has led to the present chaos. Complication without order or principle is the very definition of chaos. There is now a general realization of this fact and we only differ as to the nature of the order or principle that should be introduced. Those people who hide their lack of principle under the word realism can only conceive of a rational order of society invented by a minority (sometimes a minority of one) and imposed on the majority by force. Another party can only conceive of a moral order guaranteed by a supernatural sanction, and accepted not so much by reason as by goodness of heart. Such a moral order is the idea of a Christian society, and it is an idea that can still attract the mind as well as the heart. Its weakness is that it demands a voluntary emotional surrender, or alternatively an intuitional recognition of absolute values: it cannot appeal to any external objective standard. The way which I consider the true way of thought is based on natural laws, but instead of giving them a literal interpretation, thereby reducing mankind to the level of animal life, it allows an analogical interpretation—exactly the same kind of relationship that we have discovered between nature and art.

The laws of nature are physical laws: they can be grouped under such general terms as rhythm, proportion, balance, precision, economy, etc. These laws, which we derive from the observation of the process of the physical universe, must be applied to our social universe. To discover these laws and to live in accordance with them is a matter of individual discipline and conduct. It is possible to discover the laws by observation and measurement—the method of science. It is also possible to discover them by self-observation and meditation—the method recommended by Lao Tzu. To live in harmony with natural law—that should be our one sufficient aim. To create a society that enables the individual to pursue this aim is our political duty.

Such a society, itself reflecting the organic rhythms and balanced processes of nature, would give the individual the greatest degree of liberty consistent with a group organization. A group organization is itself a necessity only in order to guarantee this liberty. It will be a society that reduces the machinery of government to a minimum. It will safeguard itself against the rise of tyrants and will automatically destroy any form of authority which threatens the balance of its social metabolism. It will live and act as a communal unit whose only object is the provision of the material means of security and happiness. It will be governed by a final realization that happiness is only to be secured by the individual who is free to retire within himself and discover within himself that which the Taoists call the Way: the natural Truth. Such a society is anarchist.

It was noted that in aesthetics and morals, the physical analogy provided an escape from the prison of a closed system: a quantitative leap on to a new plane of consciousness or experience. But it is doubtful if the analogy can be pursued to this extreme on the social plane, which is the plane of the practical. Here we are limited by our economic and bodily needs, and the only escape from these is death, or that stasis of bodily functions practised by Buddhist monks as a preparation for death. The final leap can only be into Nirvana, into the Heaven of the Christians, or into that more ideal and less individual immortality for which I have used the symbol of the Tree of Life. This ideal immortality, which is the only kind of which I myself can entertain an expectation, does not offer any consolation to those who, because they have not found the Way, identify their existence with their idiosyncrasies. But consolation is not necessary to the man who has shed his idiosyncrasies and accepted the laws implicit in the visible and material universe. Of such a man Santayana has said: 'The eternal has absorbed him while he lived, and when he is dead his influence brings others to the same absorption, making them, through that ideal identity with the best in him, reincarnations and perennial seats of all in him which he could rationally hope to rescue from destruction. He can say, without any subterfuge or desire to delude himself, that he shall not wholly die; for he will have a better notion than the vulgar of what constitutes his being. By becoming the spectator and confessor of his own death and of universal mutation, he will have identified himself with what is spiritual in all spirits and masterful in all apprehension; and so conceiving himself, he may truly feel and know that he is eternal.'*

III

Through all the mutations of these years I have relied on a weapon which I found in my hand as soon as I was compelled to abandon my innocent vision and fight against the despairs of

* *Reason in Religion* (1905), pp. 272-3.

experience. This weapon is adamantine and invincible, like the sickle which at the beginning of legendary time Earth gave to Cronus and with which he mutilated the divine father. The Furies were born from the drops of blood which fell in that fray. An adamantine sickle was also the weapon with which Hermes armed Perseus, and with which the head of Medusa was shorn off; and it was from that raw wound that the winged Pegasus sprang to life. Such a weapon is reason, which alone can slay despair, and cut the fetters of doubt and superstition which bind us to an Ethiopian rock. But as we wield this weapon, we find that it deals not only death, but life; and that new beings, the furies and the muses of our inspiration, gather round the carnage.

I called my first book of essays *Reason and Romanticism*, and the title was at once descriptive and prophetic. In this story of the growth of my mind, every advance has been due to the exercise of the faculty of reason; but that advance is not uniform, unimpeded. It abounds in deviations and contradictions: the opposed terms of a dialectical progression. The very bases of reason, the perceptions of an unclouded intellect, are continually being contradicted by the creative fictions of the imagination, by a world of illusion no less real than the reality of our quick awareness. It is the function of art to reconcile the contradictions inherent in our experience; but obviously an art that keeps to the canons of reason cannot make the necessary synthesis. Only an art that rises above conscious reality, only a transcendent or super-real art, is adequate. In this fact lies the final and inescapable justification of romantic art, and it is to the elucidation and illustration of this truth that I have devoted my intellectual energy in the years that are now spent.

AILRED

Ailred awakes in the raw abbey
   to the flare of rivulets
      and the coal effort of the wren
the stript twigs are
   veins of jet in the bruised flesh
      of a dawn

articulate in the organic sighs
   of rot, listless leaves, amused mice
      and the massive
         roll of drencht woods

otters advance
   in silk sheaths splash oilily
      into the cold current

Wherever the word is spoken
   the virgin is there to receive it
      the moonstone a separate fire
         on her bosom
watches an eye
   open to the broken image
      of the white hills and the high
         scatter'd quails

A NORTHERN LEGION

Bugle calls coiling through the rocky valley
have found echoes in the eagles' cries:
an outrage is done on anguish'd men
now men die and death is no deedful glory.

Eleven days this legion forced the ruin'd fields, the
burnt homesteads and empty garths, the broken arches
of bridges: desolation moving like a shadow before them, a
rain of ashes. Endless their anxiety

marching into a northern darkness: approaching
a narrow defile, the waters falling fearfully
the clotting menace of shadows and all the multiple
instruments of death in ambush against them.

The last of the vanguard sounds his doleful note.
The legion now is lost. None will follow.

KIRKDALE

I, Orm the son of Gamal
found these fractur'd stones
starting out of the fragrant thicket.
The river bed was dry.

The rooftrees naked and bleach'd.
nettles in the nave and aisleways,
on the altarstone an owl's cast
and a feather from a wild dove's wing.

There was peace in the valley:
far into the eastern sea
the foe had gone, leaving death and ruin
and a longing for the priest's solace.

Fast the feather lay
like a sulky jewel in my head
till I knew it had fallen in a holy place.
Therefore I raised these grey stones up again.

WINTER DUSK

Rain-filled ruts
reflect
an apple-green sky

Into black huts
a shawled woman
shoos her hissing geese

A cold wind
insinuates
the evening star

Bleak thorns
and wassail berries
hide the sweet thrush

DIRGE

The willows now I do regret
    beside the river Rye
the sappy earth and all
    that faked autumnal fire
cool wounds upon the granular wall
    dried veins that clutch
      the indignant eaves
weep, weep
    for all will fall

as slowly as the yellow leaves
as softly as the silken sleeves
    discarded by a bridal bed
now the bright day is dead
    is dead
and we must sleep
    or die

Acknowledgements

The publishers would like to thank
the Read family, in particular Benedict
Read and Piers Paul Read, for their
assistance in the creation of this
publication.

Thanks are also due to the Ryedale Folk
Museum for the initial suggestion of the
idea and to the Herbert Read scholar
Dr Michael Paraskos for his work in
putting the anthology together.

Publisher's Note

The spelling of the River Riccal as
'Riccall' is used in accordance with
Herbert Read's original usage. It should
not be confused with the village of Riccall
near Selby.

Also available from The Orage Press

Alfred Orage and the Leeds Arts Club
1893-1923

By Tom Steele

Alfred Orage was one of those mysterious figures in our cultural history who was in his lifetime extremely influential, and after his death almost wholly forgotten.

Orage co-founded the Leeds Arts Club, possibly the only genuine manifestation of expressionism in Britain, which promoted the philosophy of Nietzsche, the mystical socialism of the early Labour movement and suffragette feminism, as well as literary and artistic modernism. And he was the first mentor of one of the most important writers on modern art of the twentieth century, Herbert Read, helping to shape his philosophy of art, and through him the direction of international modernism.

This is a reprint of the 1990 hardback edition of a book which changed perceptions of British modernism. With his highly readable writing style, Tom Steele follows Orage's career alongside the history of the Leeds Arts Club, showing that modernism in Britain was not wholly a London-centred affair.

Lightning Source UK Ltd.
Milton Keynes UK

177392UK00001B/50/P